THE WORLD'S MAJOR
PASSENGER AIRLINERS

Bill Gunston

MALLARD PRESS

An Imprint of BDD Promotional Book Company, Inc.,
666 Fifth Avenue, New York, N.Y. 10103

A SALAMANDER BOOK

Mallard Press and its accompanying design and logo are
trademarks of BDD Promotional Book Company, Inc.
666 Fifth Avenue, New York, N.Y. 10103.

© Salamander Books Ltd., 1990
129-137 York Way,
London N7 9LG,
England

First published in the United States of America in 1991
by The Mallard Press.

ISBN 0-792-45252-6

CREDITS

Managing editor: Jilly Glassborow
Editor: Lindsay Peacock
Designer: Rachael Stone
Color artwork: © Pilot Press
Typeset by: SX Composing Ltd., England
Color separation by: Scantrans Pte Ltd., Singapore
Printed by: Proost International Book Production,
Turnhout, Belgium

CONTENTS

INTRODUCTION

In 1920 the British firm Aircraft Transport & Travel flew D.H.9 airliners between London and Amsterdam, under contract to KLM, the royal Dutch airline, which had no aircraft of its own. Later, the D.H.9s were sold to KLM and in July 1921 they began operating in KLM livery, with the "Holland" registration beginning with an H. Everyone was proud of these airliners, which could carry either two passengers or one passenger and some mail. Of course, the passenger(s) had to dress up in a heavy coat, gloves and, if possible, a helmet and earplugs.

One of these D.H.9s is seen below, in front of a KLM airliner of rather later vintage. In view of the contrast it is hard to believe the 747 entered service less than 50 years after KLM received its D.H.9s.

Today, passenger airliners come in many shapes and sizes, though none are biplanes. Some people might also regret that none are flying boats. Known as boat seaplanes in the United States, this species was very important in the 1930s. This was chiefly because in those days the greatest airports were small grass fields and the only kind of airport suitable for really large aircraft was a long stretch of calm open water. A contributory factor for the flying boat's popularity was that, in an era of unreliable engines, they were somewhat safer on long overwater crossings. Why some people hanker after the return of the flying boat is that there was plenty of room for features such as "promenade decks" and dining saloons where the passengers were outnumbered by the stewards, who, of course, prepared the meals on board. Passengers were also almost outnumbered by the flight crew as well, comprising as it might a captain, first officer, navigator, one or two radio officers and at least one engineer.

This all seems light years away from today's 747-400, which is vastly more powerful yet has just two pilots, but an army of stewards (or pursers) and stewardesses is still needed to minister to the needs of 500 highly individual passengers. In fact, the latter should find little to regret in the passing of the years, for the general standard of comfort has been hugely improved. And, of

Below: Air travel progress is emphasised by a comparison of equipment used by KLM over five decades – a D.H.9 of 1921 and a 747 of 1971.

course, it is the ability of contemporary airliners to carry people en masse that has been instrumental in slashing fares to less than one-tenth of what they were 60 years ago, in real terms.

In general, today's passenger airliners fall into a small number of distinct groups. At the bottom end, not included in this book, are the types used for air taxi work. They may have two piston or turbine engines and seats for from four to nine. Then come the 19-seaters, almost all twin-turboprops, such as the Jetstream 31, Bandeirante and Do228. The 30-40 seat class are represented by the Saab 340, Shorts 360, Let-610 and Jetstream 41. Some twin-turboprops were initially offered in this class but have now been stretched to seat 50, 60 or even 70 passengers, examples being the ATR 72 and the DHC-8 Dash 8. At the upper end of the twin-turboprops is the quiet and efficient ATP.

Once one gets to the 50-passenger size, the jets begin to take over. The obvious leader in the smaller category is the new Canadair Regional Jet. Just above come several unbuilt projects (not featured in this book) such as the proposed German/Chinese MPC-75. There is then a continuous spectrum all the way up to the 747 Jumbo Jet. In the 70-130 seat category are the competitive yet strikingly different BAe 146 family and the Fokker 100. Next come the different sizes of 737 and MD-90, the latter being an example of an airliner planned for propulsion by propfans yet going into production with conventional turbofan engines. Then there is the A320 and A321, the world's newest and most efficient jetliners. In the 200-240 seat class, airlines have a choice between the A310 wide body and the tube-like 757 narrow body, both being excellent

Above: Since 1920 air travel has grown beyond belief and airliners now take-off worldwide at an average rate of five per second.

Above: As aircraft have grown in size, so too have the engines. This Pratt & Whitney turbofan is typical of the modern powerplant.

aircraft which are cleared for long overwater flights even though they are equipped with only two engines.

The pioneer jets, the 707 and DC-8, are also in the 180-250 seat class, but are being phased out from main-line passenger service. All the remaining aircraft are the so-called wide bodies, with two aisles separating the seats. In the text, numbers such as 2+3+2 mean that there is a triple seat in the centre, separated by aisles from a double seat by the window on each side. Of course, the seat layout depends on whether the operator is trying to attract First Class customers or is more intent on merely packing people in for a package holiday. Either way, it is very much a case of the passenger paying his money and taking his choice.

AIRBUS INDUSTRIE A300

SPECIFICATION: A300-600R
Origin: International (see text).
Engines: Two turbofans, either 61,500lb (27,896kg) GE CF6-80C2A5 or 58,000lb (26,309kg) PW4158
Dimensions: Span 147ft 1in (44.84m); length 177ft 5in (54.08m); wing area 2,799sq ft (260.0m^2).
Weights: Empty 170,688lb (77,423kg); max takeoff 378,535lb (171,700kg).
Performance: Cruising speed 557mph (897km/h, M 0.82) at 30,000ft (9,144m); range with 267 passengers, baggage and reserves, max wt, 4,997 miles (8,043km).
Accommodation: Typical mixed-class 267 passengers; max (subject to certification) 375; (600 Freighter) 112,519lb (51,038kg) cargo.
History: First flight (300) 28 October 1972, (600) 8 July 1983, (600R) 9 December 1987.

Below: It was Eastern's decision to buy the A300 in 1979 that at last made the world's airlines take Airbus Industrie seriously.

The A300B was, from 1967 until 1982, Airbus Industrie's only product. Once the Boeing 747 had been launched it was obviously sensible to offer the airlines a capacious widebody, or twin-aisle, aircraft, designed for shorter sectors and powered by only two of the same engines. Amazingly, hardly any operator showed any interest. For example, in 1976 over 500 narrow-body airliners were sold, burning more than twice as much fuel per seat and making far more noise, while Airbus sold just one aircraft!

At last, in 1979, Eastern Airlines in the USA agreed to try it and found it so good it bought 34. This triggered a surge of orders, boosted by progressive improvements which, without changing the aircraft's appearance (except for the addition of tiny wingtip fences), transformed its capability.

Whereas the first A300B carried 239 passengers a distance of 1,367 miles (2,200 km), today's A300-600R carries 267 a distance of just on 5,000 miles (8,046 km)! A major factor in this fantastic improvement is that General Electric (later joined by Pratt & Whitney) have increased the takeoff thrust of the engines from 49,000 lb (22,226 kg) in the first A300B1 to 61,500lb (27,896 kg) today.

Airbus is a partnership of the chief planemakers of Britain, France, Federal Germany and Spain, helped by companies in Belgium and the Netherlands. There have been both cargo and convertible passenger/cargo versions of the A300, but all current production is centred on the A300-600 and extended-range A300-600R. These have an advanced composite structure, digital avionics, "glass cockpits" in which big coloured displays take the place of traditional instruments, small drag-reducing fences on the wingtips, and the same rear fuselage as the A310 which allows two extra rows of seats to be installed. In mid-1990, the total number of firm orders for the A300 was 415, with 331 aircraft delivered.

Below: Alitalia was another early customer, with eight A300B4-203s. This aircraft, the first of the fleet, was delivered in 1980.

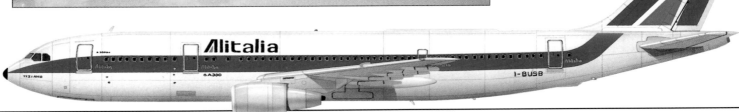

AIRBUS INDUSTRIE A310

During the mid-1970s Airbus agonised over the wish of some customers to have a smaller aircraft than the A300B. One answer was simply to put fewer seats in an A300B. The alternative seemed to be to spend millions developing a new aircraft which, though smaller, might cost more. In the event the A310 went ahead in July 1978. It has the same fuselage as the A300B but shorter. The wing, however, was designed by British Aerospace from scratch, and is of even later supercritical form than the advanced wing on the A300B.

From the start the A310 was an aircraft of outstanding aerodynamic efficiency. Like its bigger predecessor it proved amenable to progressive development in engine thrust and gross weight from 291,010lb (132,000kg) to today's figure of 346,125lb (157,000kg) so that for any given payload the range went up and up.

The A310 was launched with a choice of either the 48,000lb (21,772kg) Pratt & Whitney JT9D-7R4D or the 50,000lb (22,680kg) General Electric CF6-80A3, both installations looking very similar (and not the same as on the A300). Today, newer engines are fitted (see specification) in carbon-fibre pods hung on pylons covered in aramid-fibre composite. Many other A310 parts are also of composite materials.

Though the original Airbuses were thought of as short-haul aircraft, even the original A310-200 could carry a full passenger payload 2,844 miles

SPECIFICATION: A310-300
Origin: International (see A300 text).
Engines: Two turbofans, either 53,500lb (24,267kg) GE CF6-80C2A2 or 52,000lb (23,587kg) PW 4152
Dimensions: Span 144ft 0in (43.89m); length 153ft 1in (46.66m); wing area 2,357sq ft (219.0m²).
Weights: Empty 155,439lb (70,506kg); max takeoff 346,125lb (157,000kg).
Performance: Long-range cruising speed 543mph (875km/h, M 0.8) up to 41,000ft (12,500m); range 218 passengers, baggage and reserves, max wt, 6,160 miles (9,915km).
Accommodation: Typical mixed-class 218 passengers; max high-density 280.
History: First flight 3 April 1982, (-300) 8 July 1985.

(4,577km). What a contrast with today's Dash-300 which is being used on many of the longest intercontinental routes.

In April 1990 total sales of the A310 amounted to 85 of the Dash-200 version (all delivered) and 165 of the long-haul A310-300 (85 delivered). There is little doubt that it will continue in production throughout the 1990s.

Below: Lufthansa was the first airline to take delivery of an A310, on 7 March 1983. Today, Federal Germany's flag carrier has 10 Dash-200s and eight (of 10) Dash-300s.

Below: Wingtip fences, or winglets, distinguish all A310s built since 1985. Air India has eight Dash-300s, with General Electric CF6-80C2 engines.

9

AIRBUS INDUSTRIE A320

SPECIFICATION: A320
Origin: International (see A300 text).
Engines: Two turbofans, either 23,500-25,000lb (10,660-11,340kg) CFM56-5-A1 or 25,000lb (11,340kg) IAE V2500-A1.
Dimensions: Span 111ft 3in (33.91m); length 123ft 3in (37.57m); wing area 1,317.5sq ft (122.4m²).
Weights: Empty (fully equipped, operating) 87,634lb (39,750kg); max takeoff 162,040lb (73,500kg).
Performance: Typical long-range cruising speed 522mph (840km/h); range with 150 passengers and baggage and reserves 3,443 miles (5,541km).
Accommodation: Typical two-class 152 passengers; high-density 179 (321, two-class 186, high-density 200).
History: First flight 22 February 1987, (321) March 1993.

Below: Air Canada is taking delivery of 38 A320s with CFM56 engines. Each customer has approached this 21st-Century aircraft with apprehension, only to find it the most troublefree equipment ever.

Launched in March 1984, the A320 is a totally new design and the most advanced commercial transport in the world. Unlike such rivals as the 737 and MD-80, which are locked into fuselage and wing designs almost 30 years old, the A320 uses the very latest technology everywhere.

The wing has a supercritical section and only a 25° sweep. The fuselage width is almost exactly 13ft (3.95m), 7.5in (19cm) wider than a 737 and 24in (61cm) wider than an MD-80 or 90. The tail is made of composite material (carbon fibre except for the fin leading edge which is glass). Most significant of all, the whole aircraft is a mass of digital computers all linked to a common "data bus" network.

This enhances every part of the aircraft. If anything goes wrong, one of the displays in the cockpit will advise the pilots of the fault in any detail required. A data link conveys the information to the destination so that engineers can rectify the fault the moment the aircraft lands. The pilots fly using a small sidestick, secure in the knowledge that they cannot endanger or overstress the aircraft.

The first 21 aircraft were A320-100s, weighing 149,915lb (68,000kg). All the rest are Dash-200s, with much more fuel capacity and wingtip fences. Customers have a choice of engine. The CFM engine has an unusual four-petal thrust reverser.

The airline market soon showed that Airbus had designed a winner. From the start the A320 outsold the 737 and DC-9 at the same point in their careers. In July 1990 the total of firm orders had reached 580, with 100 delivered.

In November 1989 Airbus launched the A321, with 107 firm orders and 74 options from ten airlines. This is basically a stretched A320, 23ft (7m) longer. Though only 12% heavier it offers 24% more seats and 40% more underfloor cargo/baggage capacity. The range with 186 passengers will be 2,765 miles (4,450km). The engines will be CFM56 or V2500 rated at 31,000lb (14,060kg).

Below:Air France is one of three operators of the original A320-100s, which were the first 21 aircraft off the production line.

SPECIFICATION: A330 and A340-300
Origin: International (see A300 text).
Engines: (330) two 67,500lb (30,618kg) RR Trent, 65,500lb (29,711kg) GE CF6-80E1A1 or 64,000lb (29,030kg) PW4168; (340) four 31,200lb (14,152kg) CFM56-5C-2.
Dimensions: Span 192ft 5in (58.65m); length 208ft 10in (63.65m); wing area 3,892sq ft (361.6m²).
Weights: Empty equipped operating, (330) 257,345lb (116,730kg), (340-300) 276,680lb (125,500kg); max takeoff (330) 458,560lb (208,000kg), (340-300) 553,360lb (251,000kg).
Performance: Typical cruising speed Mach 0.82 (557mph, 897km/h); range with reserves (330, with 335 passengers) 5,310 miles (8,540km), (340 with 286 passengers) 8,700 miles (14,000km).
Accommodation: (330) 280 to 442 passengers; (340-300) 240 to about 330.
History: First flight (340-300) May 1991, (330) June 1992.

Airbus Industrie studied the A330 and A340 for ten years before deciding to go ahead in June 1987. Whereas the A310 was basically a smaller edition of the A300, the A330/340s are enlarged versions. All these aircraft use the same fuselage cross section, with a diameter of 18ft 6in (5.64m), but the larger aircraft have a totally new wing, bigger than any other wing put into production in Europe. This wing has the very latest supercritical profile, and its sweepback of 30° is 2° more than for the A300/310.

There are three versions of the new aircraft. The A330 and A340-300 are virtually identical apart from the former having two and the latter four engines, and a difference in fuel capacity (24,700 Imp gal (112,286l) for the A330 and 35,660 (162,110l) for the A340-300). Thus, the 340 is heavier, needing an extra twin-wheel landing gear under the mid-fuselage. The

Above: The first of up to 20 examples of the A330-300 (with more on option) for Trans World Airlines are scheduled to be delivered in the mid-1990s.

A340-200 is a longer-range version but with the same engines, weights and fuel capacity.

All A340s will have the same engine, a more powerful version of that fitted to the A320, installed in very low-drag pods with a full-length fan duct. A full-length duct will also be used on the extremely powerful Rolls-Royce Trent chosen by some customers for the A330, but the alternative American engines will have traditional pods.

In view of its very long range, the A340 will introduce new features to increase the efficiency and comfort of the crew. For example, flight and cabin crew can use a rest area where they can sleep in comfort, and passengers as well as crew can use an advanced com-

munications centre. This can do anything from booking a ticket for an onward connection to printing out a computerized record of bar stocks and other duty-free items, automatically kept up to date as each sale is made.

Not only are these new giants calculated to burn about 19% less fuel than any rival but further savings will come from their close similarity.

Below: Already an operator of the A300, US-based Continental Airlines plans to operate CFM56-powered A340s on some of its long-range routes.

ATR 42 & 72

SPECIFICATION: ATR 42 and 72
Origin: International, France/Italy
Engines: Two Pratt & Whitney Canada
turboprops, (42) 1,800shp (1,341kW)
PW120, (72) 2,400shp (1,788kW) PW124/2.
Dimensions: Span (42) 80ft 7.5in
(24.57m), (72) 88ft 9in (27.05m); length
(42) 74ft 4.5in (22.67m), (72) 89ft 1.5in
(27.17m); wing area (42) 586.6sq ft
(54.5m^2), (72) 656.6sq ft (61.0m^2).
Weights: Empty, operating (42) 22,674lb
(10,285kg), (72) 26,896lb (12,200kg); max
takeoff (42) 36,817lb (16,700kg), (72)
47,400lb (21,500kg).
Performance: Cruising speed, max wt (42)
279mph (450km/h), (72) 286mph
(460km/h); range with reserves (42 with
46 passengers) 1,209 miles (1,946km), (72
with 66 passengers) 1,657 miles
(2,666km).
Accommodation: (42) 42-50 passengers,
or mix passenger/cargo; (72) 64 to 74.
History: First flight (42) 16 August 1984,
(72) 27 October 1988.

*Below: An ATR 42 with Air Queensland, one
of 47 customers for the best-selling ATR
family of turboprop transports.*

A TR stands for Avions de Transport Régional, an organization set up by Aérospatiale of France and Aeritalia of Italy, both being equal partners. The first product, the ATR 42 twin-turboprop, was designed jointly. In general, the fuselage and tail is made in Italy and the wings in France, aircraft being assembled and tested at Toulouse, next door to Airbus.

The ATR 42 is a very attractive high-wing aircraft, with a T-tail and twin-wheel landing gears. Unlike the rival DHC-8, the main gears retract into fairings on each side of the tube-like fuselage, which makes them very short and light. Further weight savings come from making many parts of the aircraft from carbon-fibre composites and from Kevlar/Nomex honeycomb sandwich.

Among the Kevlar/Nomex parts are the ailerons, elevators and rudder, all of which are driven manually. The tailplane is fixed, and the flaps are simply pivoted to brackets under the wings.

Along most of the leading edges are black rubber de-icers, pneumatically inflated and deflated to break the ice off. The fuselage is fully pressurized so that on longer sectors the aircraft can cruise efficiently at 25,000ft (7,620m).

From the start of the project in November 1981 the ATR was a great commercial success. By April 1990 about 180 ATR 42s were in service all over the world, with almost another 100 on order. But in 1989 a major setback was the discovery of structural problems with the wing, and every ATR 42 has to undergo modification at ATR's expense.

Having launched the ATR 42 (the number indicating the typical number of seats) ATR next launched the ATR 72. This considerably stretched aircraft has extended wingtips with upturned fences on the ailerons, more powerful engines and considerably greater fuel capacity. Customer acceptance of this aircraft in the 72-seat class has been just as rapid as with the 42 and, by the spring of 1990, 11 were in service with another 85 on order, making a total so far for both versions of 376. This is an excellent result in a market some thought overcrowded.

*Below: In early 1990 American Eagle
operated 26 ATR 42s (as here) and
stretched ATR 72s.*

BOEING 727

SPECIFICATION: Boeing 727
Origin: USA.
Engines: Three Pratt & Whitney JT8D turbofans rated at 14,000 to 16,000lb (6,350 to 7,257kg).
Dimensions: Span 108ft 0in (32.92m); length (100) 133ft 2in (40.59m); (200) 153ft 2in (46.69m); wing area 1,700sq ft (157.9m²).
Weights: Empty (100) 80,602lb (36,561kg), (Adv 200) 102,900lb (46,675kg); max takeoff (100) 170,000lb (77,112kg), (Adv 200) 209,500lb (95,027kg).
Performance: Cruising speed 570-599mph (917-964km/h); range with max payload (100) 2,050 miles (3,300km), (Adv 200) 2,880 miles (4,635km).
Accommodation: (100) up to 131 passengers, (200) up to 189 passengers.
History: First flight (100) 9 February 1963, (200) 27 July 1967.

Above: Icelandair put this 727-108C into service in 1967. At the time it was a world-beater; today it contravenes noise regulations and burns twice as much fuel per seat as an A320!

The 727 emerged only after exceptionally prolonged studies from 1956 onwards of how to design a short-haul jet. The final configuration happened to be the same as that adopted by de Havilland for the Trident, but whereas the British aircraft was designed only for one airline, the 727 was tailored to the world market. Thus, 118 Tridents were sold (all of them now withdrawn) compared with 1,832 of the Boeing product (nearly all of which are still at work).

The original model was the 727-100, which entered service with Eastern on 1 February 1964. Incidentally, despite starting 18 months later than de Havilland, Boeing got the 727 into service with Lufthansa at the same time BEA began to use the Trident. The Dash-100 quickly suffered accidents caused by pilots letting speed decay on the approach, causing unrecoverable, excessive sink. Once pilots flew "by the book", this fast and impressive aircraft began an enviable career.

The 727 featured a cockpit resembling that of the 707, but with three throttles and engine instruments. All three engines have bucket-type reversers, that for the centre engine discharging sideways. Each main gear has twin wheels and folds inwards into the fuselage. The relatively small wing has full-span slats and Kruger flaps, and

large and very powerful triple-slotted flaps. Thus Boeing achieved the desired moderate field performance.

From the start the 727 grew in power and weight, and a QC (quick change) passenger/cargo version was added. In 1965 Boeing announced the 727-200, stretched by exactly 20ft (6.1m). This had a different arrangement of doors and emergency exits.

Total production of all versions was 1,832, ending with a batch of freighters for Federal Express in 1984. FedEx today operate a mix of 68 freighter 727s. A lot of cargo operation is at night, and the 727 cannot meet current noise legislation. In May 1990 Rolls-Royce signed a contract to refit FedEx 727s with the much quieter and fuel-efficient Tay engine. Obviously, Rolls-Royce might eventually re-engine many hundreds of 727s.

Below: Iberia of Spain bought 37 727s. This 727-256 was delivered in 1978.

The 737, "baby" of Boeing Commercial Airplanes, had a fraught beginning. Though, like the 727, it used the same cockpit and upper fuselage as the 707, it still represented a huge risk. The only customers appeared to be Eastern and Lufthansa. As Boeing's team sat down with the German airline to sign a contract for ten, Eastern announced it had picked the DC-9. Boeing almost dropped the whole idea; how could it go ahead on the basis of just ten aircraft for a foreign customer? Whoever would have thought that today, 25 years later, those ten would have been followed by 2,500 others, making the 737 the best-selling airliner of all time?

The first 30 were 737-100s, weighing 93,500lb (42,412kg) and 93ft 9in (28.58m) long. Next came the 737-200, lengthened by 6ft (1.83m) and with 16,000lb (7,258kg) engines. The engines were installed in slim nacelles attached direct to the wing with the jet-

Below: In contrast to the JT8D, the CFM56 engines of this Dash-300 are short and fat.

Above: This 737-200 displays the long but slim nacelles of the JT8D engines.

pipes and reversers aft of the trailing edge. From the 135th Dash-200, in May 1971, the standard model was the Advanced 200, with more fuel and target-type reversers which extended the nacelles a further 45in (1.14m) aft.

In March 1981 Boeing launched the 737-300, lengthened a further 8ft 8in (2.64m) and with new engines and a passenger cabin and cockpit upgraded to 757/767 standards. The CFM56 engines are hung in short pods ahead of the wing, which has extended tips.

Next came the Dash-400, further extended by a 5ft 6in (1.68m) plug ahead of the wing and a 4ft (1.22m) plug aft. There are four overwing emergency exits instead of two, and a tail bumper is added. In May 1987 Boeing launched the Dash-500, with the same body length as the discontinued -200 but with the modern features of the 300/400. Already sales of the advanced CFM-engined models exceed 1,400.

SPECIFICATION: Boeing 737
Origin: USA.
Engines: (100, 200) two P&W JT8D turbofans at 14,000 to 16,000lb (6,350 to 7,257kg); (300, 400, 500) two CFM56-3 turbofans at 18,500 to 23,500lb (8,391 to 10,660kg).
Dimensions: Span (100, 200) 93ft 0in (28.35m), (300, 400, 500) 94ft 9in (28.88m); length (100) 93ft 9in (28.58m), (200) 100ft 2in (30.53m), (300) 109ft 7in (33.4m), (400) 119ft 7in (36.45m), (500) 101ft 9in (31.0m); wing area (100) 922sq ft (85.65m^2), (200) 1,098sq ft (102m^2), (300-500) 1,135sq ft (105.4m^2).
Weights: Empty, operating (200) 60,507lb (27,445kg), (300) 69,400lb (31,479kg), (400) 73,700lb (33,430kg); max takeoff (100) 93,500lb (42,412kg), (200) 124,500lb (56,472kg), (300) 138,500lb (62,822kg), (400) 150,500lb (68,265kg), (500) up to 133,500lb (60,554kg).
Performance: Cruising speed (all) 482-532mph (775-856km/h); range with reserves (200 with 115 passengers) 2,136 miles (3,437km), (300 with 141 passengers) 2,830 miles (4,554km), (400 with 146 passengers) 2,879 miles (4,633km), (500 max weight with 108 passengers) 3,450 miles (5,552km).
Accommodation: (100) 88-107, (200) 130, (300) 149, (400) 170, (500) 108-132.
History: First flight 9 April 1967, (200) 8 August 1967, (300) 24 February 1984, (400) 19 February 1988, (500) 30 June 1989.

Popularly called the Jumbo Jet, the 747 is easily the biggest, heaviest and most powerful jetliner in the world. It has a complete segment of the market to itself, and is unlikely ever to have a competitor. It was launched by an order for 25 from PanAm on 13 April 1966. Boeing took another gigantic financial gamble with this monster. There was no certainty that orders would even reach 40. But, by the end of 1990, the 1,000th 747 will probably have been ordered. At $160,000,000 each that's a lot of business.

Features of the 747 included a repetition of the layout of the 707, with four engines widely separated along the leading edge of a sharply swept wing, sweep being 37.5°. In the 747-100 all passengers are at the same level, seated up to ten-abreast with two aisles. Up a stairway is the flight deck, aft of which could be a crew rest area, a bar and lounge or 32 seats. There are five doors on each side of the main deck. The main landing gear comprises four four-wheel bogies all stowed in the fuselage, two retracting forwards and two inwards. On the wing are very advanced high-lift slats and flaps.

The 747SR is a lightweight shorter-range version. The -200B is a stronger and heavier model, the -200C, F and M being convertible, freighter and Combi (combined) versions. The 747SP is a longer-range model with a short body, simpler flaps and a larger tail.

In 1980 Boeing announced the 747-300, with the SUD (stretched upper deck). This changes the appearance and adds 23ft 4in (7.11m) to the upper deck to seat up to 69 extra passengers. The latest, heaviest and longest-ranged model, the 747-400, has extended wings with tip fences, digital avionics and a new two-man cockpit.

SPECIFICATION: Boeing 747
Origin: USA.
Engines: Four turbofans, initially 43,500lb (19,732kg) P&W JT9D-3, later JT9D to 54,750lb (24,835kg), GE CF6-45 at 46,500lb (21,092kg) to CF6-50E2 at 52,500lb (23,814kg) or RB211 at 50,100-53,110lb (22,725-24,091kg). Current options CF6-80C2, PW4056 or RB211-524G all in 58,000lb (26,309kg) class.
Dimensions: Span 195ft 8in (59.64m), except -400 211ft 0in (64.31m); length 231ft 10in (70.66m), except SP 184ft 9in (56.31m); wing area 5,500sq ft (511m²), except -400 5,650sq ft (524.89m²).
Weights: Empty, operating (100) 348,816lb (158,223kg), (200B typical) 378,200lb (171,552kg), (SP) 333,900lb (151,454kg), (300) 390,000lb (176,901kg), (400) 391,000lb (177,354kg); max takeoff (100) 710,000lb (322,056kg), (200B, 300) 833,000lb (377,840kg), (SP) 700,000lb (317,515kg), (400) 870,000lb (394,625kg).
Performance: Cruising speed (most) 553mph (891km/h), (300) 561mph (903km/h), (400) up to 572mph (921km/h); range at econ cruise (100 with 366 passengers) 5,990 miles (9,640km), (200B with 366) 7,542 miles (12,138km), (SP with 276) 7,658 miles (12,324km), (300 with 400) 7,700 miles (12,392km), (400 with 412) 8,406 miles (13,528km).
Accommodation: (typical) up to 516 passengers, except (SP) up to 440.
History: First flight 9 February 1969, (SP) 4 July 1975, (300) 5 October 1982, (400) 29 April 1988.

Above: Delivered in 1973, G-AWNO was the 15th of a batch of 16 747-136s bought by British Airways.

Below: This aircraft of KLM is one of several 747-206Bs converted with a stretched upper deck as on the Dash-300.

BOEING 757

Throughout the 1970s Boeing studied how best to follow the 727 with an improved aircraft. Eventually the 7N7, as it was called, matured as a 727 with the original tail but a new wing, with less sweepback, and two modern turbofan engines hung under it. Shortly before the go-ahead in March 1979 Boeing redesigned the tail, and an even later change was to throw out the old cockpit and add a new nose similar to that of the 767.

The first customers were Eastern and British Airways, and for the first time Boeing launched a new airliner with a British engine (by Rolls-Royce). Regular service started on 1 January 1983, and in November 1984 the first 757

Above: Air Europe has one of the most modern jetliner fleets in the world which includes a number of 757s.

SPECIFICATION: Boeing 757
Origin: USA.
Engines: Two turbofans, either 37,400lb (16,965kg) RR 535C, 38,200lb (17,328kg) PW2037, 40,100lb (18,189kg) RR 535E4 or 41,700lb (18,915kg) PW2040.
Dimensions: Span 124ft 10in (38.05m); length 155ft 3in (47.32m); wing area 1,994sq ft (185.25m²).
Weights: Empty, operating 126,060lb (57,180kg); max takeoff 250,000lb (113,395kg).
Performance: Cruising speed Mach 0.8 (528mph, 850km/h); range with reserves (186 passengers or PF version 50,000lb, 22,680kg cargo, long-range fuel) about 4,500 miles (7,242km).
Accommodation: Up to 239 passengers.
History: First flight 19 February 1982.

Below: Singapore Airlines is one of the 29% of 757 customers who have chosen the PW2037 engine. Note the short fan cowl.

with American Pratt & Whitney engines was delivered to Delta.

Since then the two engine suppliers have fought hard. Pratt & Whitney claim their PW2000 series has lower fuel consumption, and to be the "preferred engine" – partly because it was picked for huge orders by Delta and United. Rolls-Royce, with the later E4 engine, claim much better reliability and lower costs, and so far three-quarters of 757 customers have picked the British engine.

The wing has only mild sweep (25°), but typical Boeing high-lift slats and double-slotted flaps. The main landing gears are four-wheel bogies, retracting inward, and the fuselage and cabin retain the same cross-section as the 707/727/737 family. The 757 is narrower than the A320 and Boeing claim it

offers less drag. Boeing also claim that the 757 burns less fuel per seat than any other jetliner.

Initial production aircraft were designated 757-200. When fitted with 535E4 engines it was cleared for Erops (extended-range operations) across oceans, one Air Europe aircraft being delivered non-stop from Seattle to Majorca. The 757PF (Package Freighter) is an all-cargo version, with a windowless fuselage fitted with a large side door for loading 15 cargo pallets. The -200M is a combi version with a large side door for loading cargo but retaining passenger windows.

By mid-1990 Boeing had sold about 480 of these large narrow-body airliners and delivered about 260.

BOEING 767

Above: Transbrasil bought three 767-2Q4s, delivered in 1983. They are powered by General Electric CF6-80A engines.

SPECIFICATION: Boeing 767
Origin: USA.
Engines: Two turbofans, GE CF6-80A or P&W JT9D-7R4 at 48,000 (21,773kg) or 50,000lb (22,680kg), or (later models) PW4050 to 4060 (50,000-60,000lb (22,680-27,216kg)), CF6-80C2B2/C2B6 (52,500-60,000lb (23,814-27,216kg)) or RR RB211-524H (60,000lb (27,216kg)).
Dimensions: Span 156ft 1in (47.57m); length (200) 159ft 2in (48.51m), (300) 180ft 3in (54.94m); wing area 3,050sq ft (283.3m²).
Weights: Empty, operating 177,500-198,200lb (80,512-89,902kg); max takeoff 300,000-400,000lb (136,078-181,437kg).
Performance: Cruising speed (all) Mach 0.8 (528mph, 850km/h); range, only given as "design range", varying from 3,639 to 7,836 miles (5,856-12,611km).
Accommodation: Up to 290 passengers in -200 or -300.
History: First flight (200) 26 September 1981, (300) 30 January 1986.

Like the 757, the 767 was the result of many years of study. Clearly there was a need for Boeing to produce a twin-engined wide-body to compete with the A300B and A310, and in the end it looks very like a reinvention of the Airbus aircraft. It differs mainly in having a bigger wing and narrower body. The latter obviously provides less room in the cabin and makes it impossible to use standard underfloor cargo/baggage containers, but Boeing made the decision in the interest of reduced aerodynamic drag.

The project, previously called the 7X7, was launched in July 1978, eight months before the 757. Both aircraft have almost the same cockpit with just two pilots facing electronic colour displays. The external shape of the nose, however, is quite different.

Below: Luton-based Britannia Airways also picked the General Electric CF6-80A to power its own fleet of 767-204 aircraft.

The fuselage is of almost circular section, with a maximum width of 16ft 6in (5.03m), most seating being seven-abreast. The wing sweepback is 31.5°, high-lift devices comprising full-span slats, double-slotted inboard flaps and single-slotted outboard flaps. All flight control surfaces are fully powered, and the outer wing leading edge is de-iced. The main landing gears are four-wheel bogies, retracting inwards.

The basic model is the 767-200. United flew the first service on 8 September 1982. Boeing soon also offered a medium-range model with reduced fuel capacity and an extended-range version, the -200ER, with fuel capacity increased to 20,026 Imp gal (91,038l). The 767-200ER was first sold to Ethiopian Airlines, with deliveries starting in May 1984.

In 1983 Boeing announced the 767-300 with the same takeoff weight as the -200ER but with a fuselage stretched by 21ft (6.4m), strengthened landing gear, thicker skins and other changes. This was followed in January 1985 by the -300ER, combining the longer body with additional tankage and further strengthening. By mid-1990 Boeing had sold 216 767-200s and 258 -300s.

BOEING CANADA DHC-7 (DASH 7)

DHC stands for de Havilland Canada, established in 1928 as a branch of the famous British firm. Today it is Boeing Canada, but the designations of its products have not yet been altered.

The DHC-7, or Dash 7, was launched in 1972 following a market survey into requirements for short-haul STOL (short takeoff and landing) aircraft. Making an aeroplane able to operate from a very short (say 2,500ft, 760m) airstrip obviously imposes penalties. Nobody would buy a Dash 7 and then operate it from good airports. Customers would therefore either have very

small airfields to contend with or problems with high altitudes and high ambient temperature.

Thus the Dash 7 was given a high wing with a high-lift profile, fitted with powerful double slotted flaps in the slipstream from four turboprops. The latter drive large slow-turning propellers and have twin jetpipes blowing across the wing to reduce noise. To maintain control at low airspeeds a large T-type tail is fitted, with powerful elevators and a powered double-hinged rudder, the rear rudder being hinged to the front one. The main landing gears have twin wheels and retract

forwards into the inboard engine nacelles. The wing, tailplane and engine inlets are all fitted with black pneumatic rubber deicers.

The cabin, 8ft 6in wide (2.59m), is mildly pressurized. The door is at the back, and opens to form a stairway. A customer option was a large forward cargo door to enable mixed loads to be carried, or up to five pallets in the all-cargo role.

The first service was operated by Rocky Mountain Airways of the USA on 3 February 1978. DH Canada have delivered 111 production Dash 7s, the last being completed in summer 1987.

SPECIFICATION: DHC-7
Origin: Canada.
Engines: Four 1,120shp (835kW) Pratt & Whitney Canada PT6A-50 turboprops.
Dimensions: Span 93ft 0in (28.35m); length 80ft 8in (24.58m); wing area 860sq ft (79.9m^2).
Weights: Empty, operating 27,650lb (12,542kg); max takeoff 44,000lb (19,958kg).
Performance: Cruising speed 225-261mph (362-420km/h); range with 50 passengers 840 miles (1,352km).
Accommodation: Up to 54 passengers.
History: First flight 27 March 1975.

Above: Widerøe's STOL fleet includes eight Dash-7s. They link 36 mostly small airports throughout the 1,000-mile length of Norway.

Below: Brymon is based in Plymouth, but was a pioneer of STOL services from London City Airport.

BOEING CANADA DHC-8 (DASH 8)

Above: Eastern Metro Express operates eight DHC-8-101s as well as Jetstreams on a dense network in the eastern USA.

SPECIFICATION: DHC-8
Origin: Canada.
Engines: Two P&W Canada turboprops, (100) 2,000shp (1,490kW) PW120A or 2,150shp (1,602kW) PW121, (300) 2,380shp (1,773kW) PW123.
Dimensions: Span (100) 85ft 0in (25.91m), (300) 90ft 0in (27.43m); length (100) 73ft 0in (22.25m), (300) 84ft 3in (25.68m), (400) 94ft 3in (28.73m); wing area (100) 585sq ft (54.35m²), (300) 605sq ft (56.21m²).
Weights: Empty, operating (100) 22,100lb (10,024kg), (300) 25,700lb (11,657kg); max takeoff (100) 34,500lb (15,650kg), (300) 41,100lb (18,642kg).
Performance: Cruising speed (100) 305mph (492km/h), (300) 326mph (524km/h); range with max passengers (100) 1,249 miles (2,010km), (300) 1,025 miles (1,649km).
Accommodation: (100) up to 40 passengers, (300) up to 56, (400) 70.
History: First flight (100) 20 June 1983, (300) 15 May 1987, (400) late 1992.

With the DHC-8, or Dash 8, de Havilland Canada recognized that the Dash 7 appealed only to a rather specialist market, and that a much larger number of customers would gladly trade STOL performance for either a cheaper aircraft or a higher performance. Thus, the Dash 8 was designed to use runways in the 3,500ft (1,000-1,100m) class.

Compared with the Dash 7 the new airliner is not very much smaller except in size of wing. An important difference is that almost as much power is available, but from just two engines, with lower fuel consumption. What it adds up to is that engineering and maintenance costs are reduced, and the Dash 8 flies faster on less fuel, while carrying almost as great a payload. Despite its high performance, the Dash 8 can operate with low-pressure

Below: City Express operates a high-frequency air network based at Toronto Island Airport, near the Dash-8 factory.

tyres from unpaved surfaces. The twin main wheels retract into the nacelles.

Predictably for a modern aircraft, large amounts of composite material are used in the structure, especially in the tail. Roll control is by very small manual ailerons and powered spoilers. The elevators are manual, but (as in the Dash 7) the rudder is a large powered double-hinged unit.

NorOntair flew the first service with a DHC-8 Series 100 on 19 December 1984. By April 1990 Boeing had received 236 firm orders for various sub-types of Series 100, the basic model being the Commuter, designed to fly four 115-mile (185km) sectors carrying 36 passengers and their baggage.

Judging that many customers wanted even bigger capacity, not minding a longer field length, DH Canada announced the Series 300 in 1985. This major stretch of 11ft 3in (3.43m) is accompanied by extended wingtips and a more powerful version of the PW120 engine. Deliveries began in February 1989 and over 100 of this version have now been sold. In 1990 Boeing announced specifications for the longer, heavier (55,500lb, 25,175kg) and faster Series 400.

C-GGTO

BRITISH AEROSPACE/AEROSPATIALE CONCORDE

This is one of the most famous airliners of history. Absolutely distinctive, both in appearance and (it has to be said) in noise, it is much more than twice as fast as any other of man's public transport vehicles. Sadly, instead of becoming a routine part of the equipment of airlines with long overwater routes, it was almost killed off by a wave of orchestrated protests and an enormous and unexpected rise in the price of fuel.

The project to build an SST (supersonic transport) was launched by Britain and France in November 1962. BAC (which became British Aerospace) and Sud-Aviation (which became Aérospatiale) collaborated on the airframe and systems while Bristol Siddeley (which was bought by Rolls-Royce) and the French company SNECMA worked on the slim engines.

These engines are potentially the most powerful in airline use; if they were fitted with fans their thrust would at least double. To match their operation to the enormous range of operating conditions they are installed in huge nacelles fitted with numerous inlet auxiliary doors, dump doors, variable walls and nozzles which, as well as incorporating reversers, are fully variable in size and profile. All these are extras found on no other airliner, and controlled by complex electronics, yet the reliability of Concorde has been outstanding. Another extra which could have given problems is the

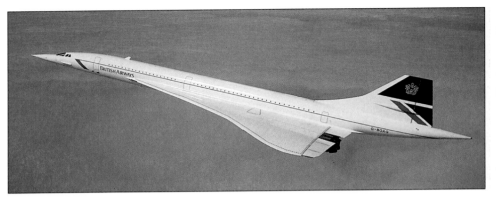

Above: G-BOAG is Concorde 214 (the 14th of the 16 production aircraft). It was withdrawn from British Airways use during the period 1982-85.

powered nose, with a sliding visor fairing mounted in a hinged nose which is lowered to give a good forward view for takeoff and landing.

Concorde's basic shape is called a 'tailless ogival delta'. Like all supersonic aircraft it has a lot of length but very little span, though because of the wing's shape it has a large area. The curved leading edge is fixed, but the trailing edge is formed by large elevons which were the first fly by wire (electrically signalled) controls on a civil transport. During acceleration from subsonic to supersonic speed the centre of lift moves back across the wing, so tons of fuel are pumped to the tail; on deceleration near the destination the fuel is pumped back. Fuel is even housed in the fin.

Fuselage width is 9ft 6in (2.9m), with luxurious 2+2 seating. The fuel capacity is 26,350 Imp gal (119,787l),

SPECIFICATION: Concorde
Origin: France/UK.
Engines: Four 38,050lb (17,259kg) Rolls-Royce/SNECMA Olympus 610 turbojets.
Dimensions: Span 84ft 0in (25.6m); length 203ft 11.5in (62.17m); wing area 3,856sq ft (358.25m²).
Weights: Empty, 170,000lb (77,110kg); max takeoff 408,000lb (185,065kg).
Performance: Cruising speed 1,353mph (2,177km/h, M 2.05); range with 100 passengers 3,870 miles (6,230km).
Accommodation: Up to 144 passengers, but normally furnished for 100.
History: First flight 2 March 1969; scheduled service from 21 January 1976.

and the cruising height is typically 57,000-60,000ft (about 18,000m).

Only 16 production aircraft were built. Services began on 21 January 1976, since when the sound of protest has faded and the supposed environment threat has become a non-event.

Below: This Concorde 101 is one of the four Concordes currently in active operation with Air France.

BRITISH AEROSPACE ONE-ELEVEN

SPECIFICATION: Rombac 1-11-560
Origin: UK (licensed to Romania)
Engines: Two 12,550lb (5,693kg) Rolls-Royce Spey 512-14DW turbofans.
Dimensions: Span 93ft 6in (28.5m); length 107ft 0in (32.61m); wing area 1,031sq ft (95.78m^2).
Weights: Empty, operating 55,704lb (25,267kg); max takeoff 104,500lb (47,400kg).
Performance: Cruising speed 472-541mph (760-870km/h); range with capacity payload and reserves 1,528 miles (2,459km).
Accommodation: Up to 109 passengers.
History: First flight (first One-Eleven) 20 August 1963, (560) 18 September 1982.

This attractive twin-jet airliner had its origins in the H.107 designed by the former Hunting Aircraft Ltd. It first flew as a product of BAC (British Aircraft Corporation), was later marketed as the BAe (British Aerospace) One-Eleven and is now produced only by IAv Bucuresti of Romania as the Rombac 1-11.

It was designed as "the jet successor to the Viscount", and the Spey engine already developed for the three-engined Trident made the project possible. The engines were hung on the rear fuselage, enabling the aircraft to sit very low on the ground, with a short and light landing gear, and powered airstairs under the tail and, as an option, at the main side door at the front. A gas-turbine APU (auxiliary power unit) is in the tailcone.

The wing is swept at only 20°, and has a fixed leading edge (de-iced by hot air bled from the engines) and Fowler flaps. The ailerons are manually operated via servo tabs, but the spoilers, lift dumpers, elevators and rudder are all hydraulically powered. A stick-pusher is fitted to avoid any "deep stall" problems, which can otherwise hit T-tailed jets with rear-mounted engines.

The One-Eleven was designed for about 65 passengers, and the first model, the Series 200, could seat 79 in a high-density layout. BAC built 56 of these, followed by nine Series 300s with uprated engines and a centre-section tank to extend the range. Then followed 69 Series 400s tailored to the US market, with numerous features demanded by FAA (Federal Aviation Administration) certification.

BEA, predecessor of British Airways, then bought the stretched Series 500, the first production example flying in February 1968. This was stretched from 93ft 6in to 107ft (28.5m – 32.6m), enabling up to 119 passengers to be carried. BAe built 87 of various types of Series 500, plus nine Series 475s.

In 1981 manufacture was transferred to Romania, since when two chief

Above: British Airways inherited One-Elevens from both BEA and British Caledonian.

models have been produced. These are the Series 495, an upgraded 475, and the 560, an upgraded 500, normally certificated for 109 passengers. IAv has been working on an initial batch of 22 aircraft.

Many One-Elevens have been fitted with silencers, which extend the rear of the engine pods (see profile). At much greater cost aircraft could be re-engined with the Rolls-Royce Tay, which would not only be much quieter but also greatly improve climb and range. In 1990 IAv Bucuresti was considering producing new aircraft with this engine. The Dee Howard '1-11 2400' Tay conversion flew in July1990.

Below: Since 1981 One-Eleven production has been carried out by IAv Bucuresti of Romania. The example shown is a Series 525FT, similar to the 560.

Left: Though wearing the livery of Continental Express, this 146-200 is one of eight bought by Presidential for US regional networks.

SPECIFICATION: BAe 146.
Origin: UK.
Engines: Four 6,970lb (3,162kg) Textron Lycoming ALF502R-5 turbofans.
Dimensions: Span 86ft 0in (26.21m); length (100) 85ft 11.5in (26.2m), (200) 93ft 10in (28.6m), (300) 101ft 8.3in (30.99m); wing area 832sq ft (77.3m²).
Weights: Empty, operating (100) 49,559lb (22,479kg), (200) 51,294lb (23,266kg), (300) 53,951lb (24,471kg); max takeoff (100) 84,000lb (38,102kg), (200) 93,000lb (42,184kg), (300) 97,500lb (44,225kg).
Performance: Cruising speed (100, 200) 416-477mph (669-767km/h), (300) 434-491mph (699-789km/h); range with max payload and reserves (100) 1,077 miles (1,733km), (200) 1,355 miles (2,179km), (300) 1,253 miles (2,020km).
Accommodation: (100) 82-93 passengers, (200) up to 112, (300) up to 128; (QT) up to 27,535lb (12,489kg) cargo.
History: First flight (100) 3 September 1981, (200) 1 August 1982, (production 300) June 1988.

This unusual airliner attracted criticism and even scorn when it appeared and, like most British aircraft, it found few customers. Then, as its qualities became better understood, it was gradually recognized as an aircraft combining many unique qualities, and the order-book grew rapidly.

It was specially designed for operations from short runways, including those in hot or high-altitude locations or hemmed in by mountains. It is loved by its pilots and is delightful to fly. It is by far the quietest jet, and almost certainly the quietest large passenger aircraft ever built. Its fuselage width of 11ft 8in (3.56m) also results in a capacious cabin which can seat six-abreast, with a perfect view from the windows.

The engines are geared turbofans, so small that fan or turbine modules could be packaged into under-floor holds. The twin-wheel landing gears all retract into the fuselage. The tail end of the fuselage is formed by large airbrakes. The ailerons and elevators are manual, but the roll spoilers and rudder are powered.

The initial 146-100 entered service with Dan-Air in May 1983. The 146-200 was extended by five frames to carry more passengers and 35% more underfloor cargo/baggage. This was first bought by Air Wisconsin which began operations in June 1983, and the same airline launched the 146-300 which was stretched even further. British Aerospace has also developed the 146-QT Quiet Trader freighter, 146-QC quick-change passenger/cargo version, Statesman VIP aircraft and a range of military variants.

In mid-1990 firm orders for the 146 totalled 213 for 41 customers all over the world. Another 80 are on option.

Below: Dan-Air was one of the first operators of the 146. It has three Dash-100s, and has now also bought the stretched Dash-300.

G-BKMN

DAN-AIR LONDON

BRITISH AEROSPACE 748 & ATP

Left: CS-TAO is one of four 748s belonging to SATA of Portugal, an airline which, over the years, has also leased several other 748s

As well as having new engines, driving quiet slow-turning six-blade propellers, the ATP is stretched considerably to provide typical seating for 64 passengers to match development of the regional airline industry.

The fuselage is pressurized to the same level (5.5 lb/sq in, $387g/cm^2$) as the 748 but is 16ft 6in (5.03m) longer and has the large elliptical windows replaced by a larger number of small rectangular ones, which is just what rival company Fokker did at the same time (F27 to F50). There are passenger doors at the front and rear, the forward door having an airstair, and front and rear above-floor baggage compartments with doors on the right. Unlike the 748 the rudder is power assisted. The centre section and Fowler flaps are wider, but the pneumatic deicers are little changed.

It is strange that, though it is the quietest of all the modern turboprops, and certainly has the lowest cost per seat-mile, the ATP has sold in only small numbers. Service began in May 1988 with British Midland. By mid-1990 orders for the ATP totalled only a modest 39.

SPECIFICATION: ATP
Origin: UK.
Engines: Two 2,653shp (1,977kW) Pratt & Whitney Canada PW 126 turboprops.
Dimensions: Span 100ft 6in (30.63m); length 85ft 4in (26.0m); wing area 842.8sq ft ($78.3m^2$).
Weights: Empty, operating 31,390lb (14,238kg); max takeoff 50,550lb (22,930kg).
Performance: Cruising speed 272-306mph (437-493km/h); range with 64 passengers and reserves 1,134 miles (1,825km).
Accommodation: Seating for 60-72 passengers.
History: First flight (748) 24 June 1960, (ATP) 6 August 1986.

Below: LIAT (Leeward Islands Air Transport) had an option on four ATPs. Another customer is SATA, which is buying three to replace its BAe 748s (see above).

Today's ATP (Advanced Turbo Prop) is a completely updated development of the 748. This latter aircraft was designed in the late 1950s as the Avro 748, was produced in the 1960s as the Hawker Siddeley 748 and is now flying as the British Aerospace 748. Though powered by the same engines as the Handley Page Herald and Fokker F27, it differed from these rivals in being a low-wing aircraft. The final basic version was the 748 Series 2B, with extended span, uprated engines, improved tail surfaces and other less obvious refinements.

During the 1970s it was increasingly obvious that, though tough and reliable, the Dart engine's 1945 technology was completely outmoded. To remain in the market, British Aerospace had to switch to a modern engine, and on 1 March 1984 the ATP was announced.

The Caribbean Airline

liat

BRITISH AEROSPACE JETSTREAM

SPECIFICATION: Jetstream
Origin: UK.
Engines: Two Garrett turboprops (31) 940shp (700kW) TPE331-10UG, (Super 31) TPE331-12 flat-rated at 1,020shp (760kW), (41) TPE331-14 flat-rated at 1,500shp (1,118kW).
Dimensions: Span 52ft 0in (15.85m); (41) 60ft 0in (18.29m); length 47ft 1.5in (14.37m), (41) 63ft 5in (19.33m); wing area 271.3sq ft (25.2m^2), (41) 350sq ft (32.5m^2).
Weights: Empty, operating (31) 9,894lb (4,488kg), (S31) 10,092lb (4,578kg), (41) 13,544lb (6,144kg); max takeoff (31) 15,322lb (6,950kg), (S31) 16,204lb (7,350kg), (41) 22,377lb (10,150kg).
Performance: Cruising speed (31) 264-303mph (426-488km/h), (S31) 281-304mph (452-489km/h), (41) 334-339mph (537-546km/h); range with reserves (31 with 18 passengers) 783 miles (1,260km), (S31 with 19 passengers) 805 miles (1,296km), (41 with 29 passengers) 679 miles (1,093km).
Accommodation: (Super 31) up to 19 passengers, (41) up to 29.
History: First flight 18 August 1967, (31) 18 March 1982, (41) June 1991.

Like many British aircraft, the Jetstream has had a chequered history which began haltingly and gradually turned into a worldwide smash hit. Now, joined by a stretched version, the Jetstream has become very successful.

The Jetstream was designed by Handley Page Ltd in the 1960s. When this company went bankrupt the Jetstream was taken over by Scottish Aviation, but this company in turn was absorbed into British Aerospace. At last, in December 1978, BAe decided to go ahead with a new version called the Jetstream 31. This replaced the Astazou engines by American Garretts and introduced numerous refinements.

The first deliveries in 1982 were to customers in Germany and Britain, but the biggest market was in the USA where the fast Fairchild Metro was already entrenched. In time, however, the much greater comfort and ''stand-up'' headroom of the J31 proved so attractive that by mid-1990 no fewer than 250 were serving with 15 US local airlines.

The four basic models are the J31 Airliner, Executive Shuttle, Corporate and Special Role. The Super 31 has more powerful engines, higher performance and an improved cabin.

BAe's Scottish factory at Prestwick is now working with partners Field Aircraft and Pilatus of Switzerland on the Jetstream 41. The J41 will have a fuselage 16ft (4.88m) longer which will be mounted entirely above the wing, the two parts being joined in a huge wing/body fairing.

Above: Australian (formerly Trans-Australia) bought three Jetstream 31s in 1985. Today's Australian users are Eastern and Skywest.

Below: Mall Airways of New York bought the second production Jetstream 31.

CANADAIR REGIONAL JET

In recent years there has been such a fantastic upsurge of interest in twin-turboprops for local-service and regional airlines that it came as quite a shock when Canadair and Shorts both proposed small twin-jets. Shorts was first, offering the "clean sheet of paper" FJX in March 1988. This would have been an excellent aircraft, but it was killed off when Shorts was purchased by the rival Canadair. This left just the Canadian company's RJ, which is compromised by having the same fuselage diameter (less spacious than the FJX) inherited from the Challenger business jet.

The Regional Jet is basically a Challenger 601 with a stronger structure, slightly extended wingtips with winglets, extra spoilers, and a fuselage stretched by 20ft (6.10m) to more than double the seating capacity. There are

Below: As soon as Shorts became Canadian owned British Airways ordered a fleet of RJs.

Above: This artist's impression shows how the prototype Canadair Regional Jet will probably be painted when it flies in 1991.

many other minor changes, but the RJ is still a stretched Challenger, with exactly the same engines.

As a business aircraft the Challenger is excellent, but the fuselage diameter of 8ft 10in (2.69m) is similar to that of older turboprops such as the Fokker F27 and BAe 748, and 1ft (0.3m) less than newer four-abreast aircraft such as the multi-national N-250 turboprop and MPC-75 jet which are planned for the late 1990s. The cabin will actually be 7ft 2in (2.18m) wide at floor level and have a centreline headroom of 6ft 1in (1.85m). The pressurization will be to 8.3lb/sq in (584g/cm^2), compared with 9 (633) for the Challenger, reflecting the lower normal cruise altitude of up to 36,000ft (10,973m) though the RJ will be cleared to 41,000ft (12,497m), which would seldom be reached.

Though maximum weight is appreciably heavier than a Challenger, this is made up of extra structure and payload. Fuel capacity is sharply reduced, from 2,041 Imp gal to 1,166 (9,278-5,300l). All flight control surfaces are fully powered, and the tailplane is electrically driven for trimming. The flaps are double-slotted, and the fixed wing leading edge has thermal deicing. The engines have cascade-type reversers in the fan ducts. All units of the short landing gear have twin wheels.

SPECIFICATION: Regional Jet
Origin: Canada.
Engines: Two 9,220lb (4,182kg) GE CF34-3A turbofans.
Dimensions: Span 70ft 4in (21.44m); length 88ft 5in (26.95m); wing area 520sq ft (48.31m^2).
Weights: Empty, operating 30,100lb (13,653kg); max takeoff 47,450lb (21,523kg).
Performance: Cruising speed 488-529mph (786-851km/h); range at 488mph with 50 passengers 1,005 miles (1,617km).
Accommodation: Up to 50 passengers.
History: First flight mid-1991.

Shorts are responsible for the fuselage section, front and rear extension plugs, flaps, ailerons, and outboard "spoilerons" (serving as airbrake/spoilers). These are shipped from Belfast to the assembly line at Montreal.

EMBRAER EMB-110 BANDEIRANTE

SPECIFICATION: Bandeirante
Origin: Brazil.
Engines: Two 750shp (559kW) Pratt &
Whitney Canada PT6A-34 turboprops.
Dimensions: Span 50ft 3.5in (15.33m);
length 49ft 6.5in (15.10m); wing area
313.23sq ft (29.1m²).
Weights: Empty, operating 7,915lb
(3,590kg); max takeoff 13,010lb (5,900kg).
Performance: Cruising speed 212-256mph
(341-411km/h); range with max passengers
308 miles (497km).
Accommodation: P1A, quick-change cabin
for 18 passengers, (P2A) up to 21.
History: First flight 26 October 1968,
(current P1A, P2A) 1983.

Starting from nothing on 2 January 1970, Brazil's Embraer has worked its way to becoming one of the world's leading planemakers. It has already delivered well over 4,000 aircraft. Some have been foreign designs made under licence, but many have been designed at the factory at Sao José dos Campos. One of the most successful is this small twin-turboprop.

A straightforward low-wing machine, the EMB-110 Bandeirante (Pioneer) has an airframe almost entirely of metal, with glassfibre wingtips, wing/body fairing and dorsal fin. The cabin is unpressurized and thus can have almost flat sides. There are doors at both front and rear on the left, the rear for passengers and the front for crew and, optionally, for passengers also. The floor is stressed for cargo and in the EMB-110K or -110P1K the rear door is 5ft 11in (1.8m) wide for loading bulky cargo. The Air Ecosse aircraft depicted below has such a door. Embraer has also sold various other versions for crew training, paradropping, search/rescue and aeromedical evacuation. In the latter role there is room for six stretchers.

Since 1983 Bandeirantes have incorporated various updates, the most obvious being a tailplane with dihedral. Designated EMB-110P1A and P2A, these have now been followed by the P1A/41 and P2A/41, certified at the increased weight given in the specification.

Customers have many options, mainly concerning avionics and equipment. Among these are a Collins EFIS (electronic flight instrument system), Bendix autopilot and weather radar.

The first customer aircraft was delivered on 9 February 1973. Since then Embraer has produced almost exactly 500 Bandeirantes, sold to 80 customers in 36 countries.

Left: Approximately three-quarters of the 500 or so Bandeirantes now in service are operated by quite small local-service operators, appreciative of the Brazilian aircraft's economic flying costs.

Below: Another parcel carrier is, of course, the United Kingdom's Post Office. Embraer Bandeirantes are operated, mainly at night, by Air Ecosse.

EMBRAER EMB-120 BRASILIA

SPECIFICATION: Brasilia
Origin: Brazil.
Engines: Two 1,800shp (1,341kW) Pratt & Whitney Canada PW118 turboprops.
Dimensions: Span 64ft 10.7in (19.78m); length 65ft 7.5in (20.0m); wing area 424.42sq ft (39.43m^2).
Weights: Empty, operating 15,586lb (7,070kg); max takeoff 25,353lb (11,500kg).
Performance: Cruising speed 299-343mph (482-552km/h); range with reserves (30 passengers) 1,088 miles (1,750km).
Accommodation: Up to 30 passengers.
History: First flight 27 July 1983.

The global success of the Bandeirante enabled Embraer to market the fast, pressurized Xingu and then the EMB-120 Brasilia. This has also been followed by two even later machines, the EMB-145 Amazon with two turbofans and the CBA-123 with twin pusher turboprops mounted at the tail which is being developed jointly with FAMA of Argentina. If all succeed, Embraer could become No 1 in local-service airliners.

Design of the Brasilia began in September 1979, and Embraer claimed it would be the fastest of the new generation of turboprop passenger aircraft. Like the Bandeirante it is a conventional low-wing aircraft but distinguished by a T-tail. Structure is metal except for leading edges, tips and fairings which are of Kevlar-reinforced glassfibre. Unlike the Bandeirante the Brasilia has twin-wheel main gears retracting forward and a pressurized

Above: Though wearing Air France titles this Brasilia is one of three operated by Air Littoral, which is based at Montpellier on the Mediterranean.

cabin. It also naturally has far more power, but the propellers still have only four blades.

Again unlike the Bandeirante, the fact that the Brasilia is pressurized means that the fuselage is a tube, the maximum cabin width of 6ft 10¹¹⁄₁₆in (2.10m) being achieved well above floor level. Unlike some local-service airliners the fuselage sits on top of the wing so that the spars do not form an obstructive step in the cabin, and this is especially important as headroom is only 5ft 9in (1.75m). Seating is three-abreast (2+1), and the main door, used by both crew and passengers, opens out and down to form an airstair. The large door at the back serves the pressurized baggage compartment. Ailer-

rons and elevators are manual but the rudder comprises front and rear dual-hinged units with full hydraulic power. The hydraulics also drive the landing gear and double-slotted Fowler flaps.

By the spring of 1990 orders and options for this fast commuter airliner totalled almost 450. The first customer, ASA, received its first aircraft at the 1985 Paris air show, and a year later United Technologies took delivery of an 18-seat VIP example of the Corporate version.

Below: The first Brasilia to be delivered was one of a fleet of 35 for Atlantic Southeast Airlines, based at Atlanta, Georgia.

Between the World Wars Fokker of Amsterdam was one of the world's leading builders of airliners. But in 1945 it faced a shattered factory, new technologies and soaring development costs. How could it, with a miniscule home market, compete with the USA and claw back its place in the market?

It did it with a project initially called P.275 in 1952. Showing amazing foresight, the company picked the Rolls-Royce Dart turboprop, an engine already in production for the Viscount, and making a name for itself in a world which had previously used only piston engines and high-octane petrol. Other features of the P.275 were a high wing, made small for speed rather than big for short field length, and a pressurized cabin seating 32 passengers who enjoyed a panoramic view through elliptical picture windows (another feature taken from the Viscount). As the F27 Friendship, the prototype flew in November 1955.

Gradually it found customers. Then, remarkably, it was picked by Fairchild for licence production in the USA; in fact, it was a Fairchild F27 – with nose radar and seating 40 – that flew the first service in 1958. Just 20 years later the last F27 was delivered to the last of 168 customers in 63 countries. The sales total of 786 far exceeds that of any other West European airliner.

Since 1970 Fokker had been hoping Rolls-Royce would produce a new engine. Eventually, in November 1983, the company went ahead with the Fokker 50 (the number indicates

Above: For many years Sudan Airways has operated two F27-200s from Khartoum and has also used a -400M. Orders have now been placed for the F50.

standard seating) with a Canadian engine. Fokker was, however, able to stay with the British firm Dowty Rotol. This company supplies the landing gears, the twin-wheel main units which retract backwards into the long nacelles, and the very efficient low-noise propellers, each with six composite blades. Apart from these and the engines, almost the only other visible new feature in the F50 is the switch to numerous small 'Boeing type' passenger windows.

Fokker brought in companies in Belgium, West Germany, France and Japan to assist with making the F50, as it could not have handled production of the F50 and the F100 alone. By May 1990, orders and options for the 50 had already passed the 180 mark. A 68-seat version is planned.

SPECIFICATION: Fokker 50
Origin: Netherlands.
Engines: Two 2,500shp (1,863kW) Pratt & Whitney Canada PW125B turboprops.
Dimensions: Span 95ft 1.7in (29.0m); length 82ft 10in (25.25m); wing area 753.5sq ft (70m²).
Weights: Empty, operating 27,712lb (12,570kg); max takeoff 45,900lb (20,820kg).
Performance: Cruising speed 325mph (522km/h); range with 50 passengers and reserves 1,732 miles (2,787km).
Accommodation: 46-58 passengers.
History: First flight 28 December 1985.

Below: Luxembourg's airline, for many years an F27 operator, has now ordered three Fokker F50s, with another three on option.

FOKKER F28 & 100

Having in the early 1950s taken a giant gamble with the F27 turboprop, Fokker then took a much bigger one in the early 1960s with a jet. The Caravelle, One-Eleven and DC-9 were already entrenched, so how could Fokker find a niche? The answer was to aim lower, at the 55- to 65-seat class.

Thus, the F28 Fellowship, first flown on 9 May 1967, was powered by slightly simpler and lower-powered versions of the same Spey engine as used in the One-Eleven. The wing was given hardly any sweepback, short field length being judged more important than speed. At the back was a T-type tail and a pair of large airbrakes forming the fuselage tailcone.

Despite being a latecomer with hardly any home market, Fokker achieved great success with the F28. Later versions seated up to 85 passengers and had slatted wings of increased span and other improvements. When production came to an end in 1986, Fokker had sold 241 F28s to 57 customers in 37 countries.

For several years Fokker studied the prospects for the F29, an altogether bigger aircraft strongly resembling the A320 but with a T-tail. Eventually, in 1983, the Amsterdam firm announced it was going ahead with the Fokker 100, the number indicating a typical passenger capacity. Unlike the F29, the F100 is a stretched and updated F28

Below: The Fokker 100's breakthrough into the US market came in July 1985 when US Air ordered 20, plus another 20 on option.

Above: Piedmont was one of very few major carriers to buy the F28, with a fleet of 20 F28-1000s and eight leased Dash-4000s.

with new engines and a new wing of advanced transonic profile. Other updates include a digital flight system and "glass cockpit" displays. Many airframe parts are made of advanced fibre-reinforced composite materials, or of honeycomb construction.

Fokker put together a collaborative manufacturing package. Some fuselage sections and the complete tail are made by MBB in West Germany. The wings are made by Shorts in Northern Ireland, and the aft-mounted engine nacelles and thrust reversers are made by Grumman near New York. As with the F50, Dowty Rotol make the neat twin-wheel landing gears in England, and the engines, which are more fuel-efficient than the Spey and also meet all existing and future noise legislation without needing silencing nozzles, come from Derby, England.

SPECIFICATION: Fokker 100
Origin: Netherlands.
Engines: Two Rolls-Royce Tay turbofans, 13,850lb (6,282kg) Mk 620-15 or 15,100lb (6,849kg) Mk 650-15, with option of 18,000lb (8,165kg) Mk 670.
Dimensions: Span 92ft 1.5in (28.08m); length 116ft 6.8in (35.53m); wing area 1,006.4sq ft (93.5m^2).
Weights: Empty 53,738lb (24,375kg); max takeoff 98,000lb (44,450kg).
Performance: Cruising speed (max) 508mph (818km/h); range (107 passengers, auxiliary tank, Mk 650 engines) 1,756 miles (2,826km).
Accommodation: Normal 107 passengers, max 122.
History: First flight 30 November 1986.

The first F100 flew in 1986 and this 107-seat version was first delivered in February 1988. By the spring of 1990 total orders were approaching the 400 mark. Fokker is studying shorter and longer versions.

ILYUSHIN Il-62

SPECIFICATION: Il-62M
Origin: Soviet Union.
Engines: Four 24,250lb (11,000kg) Soloviev D-30KU turbofans.
Dimensions: Span 141ft 9in (43.2m); length 174ft 3.5in (53.12m); wing area 3,009sq ft (279.55m²).
Weights: Empty, operating 153,000lb (69,400kg); max takeoff 363,760lb (165,000kg).
Performance: Cruising speed 509-560mph (820-900km/h); range (max payload of 50,700lb, (23,000kg), with reserves) 4,846 miles (7,800km).
Accommodation: 140 mixed-class passengers or up to 170 economy.
History: First flight January 1963.

In the early 1960s the only long-range airliner available to the Soviet airline Aeroflot was the propeller-driven Tu-114. Clearly there was a need for a jet, and the task fell on the design bureau of S.V.Ilyushin at Khodinka. The result, the Il-62, was almost identical in form to the British VC10.

The low wing is swept at 32.5° and carries slotted flaps and large manually driven ailerons but has a fixed leading edge. Most unusually, the T-type tail has both elevators and the rudder driven manually, though for trimming purposes the tailplane is driven electrically. All leading edges are de-iced by hot air. In the first prototype, which flew in January 1963, the engines were Lyulka Al-7 turbojets, hung on the rear fuselage. In the first production version, which entered service between Moscow and Montreal in September 1967, the engines were 23,150lb (10,500kg) Kuznetsov NK-8-4s.

Above: The biggest operator of the Il-62 family is the Soviet Union's Aeroflot which has about 180. This example is an Il-62M.

First seen in 1971, the Il-62M is an improved version with engines which are both more powerful and also more fuel-efficient (see specification). The improved efficiency extends the range, and this is improved still further by making the fin a fuel tank as in the Super VC10. The new engine nacelles have larger inlets, improved streamline shape and more effective clamshell reversers. Other improvements include the use of the spoilers to augment roll control and the introduction of a containerised baggage and cargo system. Improvements were also made to the flight deck and avionics. The Il-62M entered service on the Moscow-Havana route in 1974 and progressively took over all Aeroflot's long-distance routes.

In 1978 the Il-62MK was announced. This retains the same dimensions and engines, but has strengthened wings, wider main landing-gear four-wheel bogies, lower-pressure tyres, improved non-skid brakes and revised spoilers which flick open automatically on landing to kill wing lift. Maximum weight is cleared to 368,170lb (167,000kg) and the main passenger cabin has a wide-body look with indirect lighting and enclosed overhead baggage racks. This version is cleared to carry 195 passengers. About 250 Il-62s were produced.

Below: CSA Czech airlines was the first non-Soviet operator with five Il-62s (shown here), later followed by six Il-62Ms.

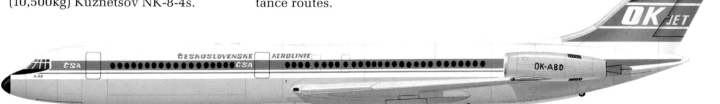

ILYUSHIN Il-86

Throughout the early 1970s Aeroflot and the Ilyushin design bureau studied how best to build the Soviet Union's first wide-body passenger transport. Should it have two decks or two fuselage 'tubes' side by side? Should the engines be at the back or under the wing? In the end, when construction went ahead in 1986, the Il-86 was rather like a slightly smaller 747 but with the cockpit in the nose instead of at an upper level.

The wing is swept at 35° and has full-span leading-edge slats as well as double slotted flaps and powered spoilers. All control surfaces are powered, the rudder and elevators being in two sections.

The engines are advanced versions of those fitted to the original Il-62 and Tu-154. They are hung on pylons under the wing. There is a fence across the top of the wing behind each pylon, and each engine has a combined reverser and noise reducer. Though bigger than an Il-62, the Il-86 has a smaller fuel capacity because its range is lower. It was planned to fly 5,000km (3,107 miles), but in practice proved unable to do this. Accordingly, the Il-96 was developed, but the Il-86 still remains very important.

It is the most capacious passenger aircraft ever built in the Soviet Union. In the original Aeroflot Il-86 passengers board via any of three large powered staircases extended from the left side of the lower deck. There they leave their coats and baggage and then walk up three large fixed internal staircases to the upper deck where the seats are. In an alternative version passengers can board via airport jetties to four doors on the main deck. Doing away with the lower-deck doors and stairways enables 25 more passengers to be carried. This version can carry 16 LD3 cargo containers instead of eight.

SPECIFICATION: Il-86
Origin: Soviet Union.
Engines: Four 28,660lb (13,000kg) Kuznetsov NK-86 turbofans.
Dimensions: Span 157ft 8in (48.06m); length 195ft 4in (59.54m); wing area 3,444sq ft (320m^2).
Weights: Empty, operating, not published (max payload 42 tonnes, max fuel 86 tonnes); max takeoff 458,560lb (208,000kg).
Performance: Cruising speed 559-590mph (900-950km/h); range (max payload) 1,553 miles (2,500km).
Accommodation: Up to (standard all nine-abreast) 350 passengers.
History: First flight 22 December 1976.

Above: SSSR-86009 is one of an estimated 75 Il-86 wide-bodies in service with Aeroflot. Because of failure to meet range requirements some or all may be re-engined.

Below: Aircraft No 86000 was the prototype, first flown in 1976. Externally it looked much like the aircraft now in service, but problems have been prolonged.

ILYUSHIN Il-96

When news of the Il-96 reached the West in 1986 it was assumed that it was just a re-engined Il-86. In fact, though it has the same fuselage cross-section and uses the same landing gear and generally similar systems, the Il-96 is a completely fresh design. It was developed to overcome the deficiency in range of the Il-86 and the only known version is the Il-96-300.

The Ilyushin designers appear to have copied a Western team in the wing, which is almost identical to that of the 747 except that it is slightly smaller. Like the 747-400, the wing also has tip fences (winglets). The designers are also copying Airbus in developing a twin-engined as well as a four-engined version of the aircraft. The giant twin will have Lotarev D-18T engines of between 61,750 and 70,500lb (28,000 and 32,000kg) thrust.

SPECIFICATION: Il-96-300
Origin: Soviet Union.
Engines: Four 35,275lb (16,000kg) Soloviev PS-90A turbofans.
Dimensions: Span 189ft 2in (57.66m); length 181ft 7.3in (55.35m); wing area 4,215sq ft (391.6m^2).
Weights: Empty, operating 257,940lb (117,000kg); max takeoff 476,200lb (216,000kg).
Performance: Cruising speed 528-559mph (850-900km/h); range (66,140lb, (30,000kg) payload, plus reserves) 5,590 miles (9,000km).
Accommodation: Three-class 235 passengers, all-tourist 234+66 (many more could be accommodated).
History: First flight 28 September 1988.

The four engines of the Il-96 are of the new PS-90A type, also used for the Tu-204. These are much more fuel-efficient than the engines of the Il-86, besides being considerably quieter.

Apart from the better engines, the chief reason for the much greater range of the Il-96-300 is that its fuel capacity is approximately doubled. Normal capacity of the integral wing tanks of the Il-86 is 15,398 Imp gal (70,000l), whereas that of the Il-96 is no less than 33,572 Imp gal (152,618l). This is the reason for the newer airliner's greater maximum takeoff weight.

In fact, despite its much bigger wing, the structure of the Il-96-300 actually weighs rather less than that of the Il-86. This is partly because of increased use of low-density composite materials, and partly because the fuselage is somewhat shorter.

The prototype Il-96-300 made its first flight on 28 September 1988. In the Soviet Five-year Plan for 1990-95 it was intended that 70 should be built. Aeroflot had, by 1988, ordered over 100 and CSA of Czechoslovakia had also expressed interest, before deciding to buy the Airbus A310.

Left: By mid-1990, only the first Il-96-300 had been seen, though the aircraft has often been demonstrated in public.

Below: This profile of the Il-96-300 shows the PMKB (Soloviev) badge and 'PS-90A' inscribed on each pod.

LET L-410 & L-610

It was in 1966 that the Czech Let company began to design a twin-turboprop airliner, the L-410 Turbolet. It had a high wing mounted above a fuselage of circular section but without pressurization. All three units of the landing gear have single wheels, the main units retracting into blister fairings on the flanks of the fuselage. All flight controls are manual, the elevators and rudder being fabric covered. Some complexity was accepted in order to get short field performance, the wing having hydraulically driven double-slotted flaps.

The Motorlet (Walter) factory could not produce the M601 engine in time, so the prototype made its first flight on 16 April 1969 powered by Canadian PT6A engines. Let built 31 with this engine, plus a special photo version for Hungary. The Let-410M, with the Czech M601 engine, followed in 1973, and 110 of these were built, mainly for Aeroflot in the Soviet Union.

From 1979 the standard model was the Let-410UVP, with a longer fuselage, greater wingspan, dihedral tailplane, bigger fin and rudder, improved cockpit and avionics, and other changes. It had to be able to operate in temperatures as low as −76°F (-60°C). Let delivered 495 UVP versions, following in 1985 with the UVP-E with extra tanks on the wingtips and seating increased from 15 to 19. By mid-1990 Let had delivered 255 of these.

SPECIFICATION: L-410UVP-E
Origin: Czechoslovakia.
Engines: Two 750-809shp (559-603kW) Motorlet M 601E turboprops.
Dimensions: Span (over tip tanks) 65ft 6.5in (19.98m); length 47ft 4in (14.43m); wing area 378.67sq ft (35.18m^2).
Weights: Empty, operating, 8,785lb (3,985kg); max takeoff 14,110lb (6,400kg).
Performance: Cruising speed 227-236mph (365-380km/h); range (max cruise, with max payload and reserves) 339 miles (546km).
Accommodation: Normally 19 passengers.
History: First flight 16 April 1969, (UVP) 1 November 1977, (E) 30 December 1984.

On 28 December 1988 the prototype L-610 made its maiden flight. This is a larger aircraft, with accommodation for 40 passengers in a pressurized fuselage. The engines are M602s, each of 1,822shp (1,357kW) and driving a five-blade propeller. The wing has a span of 84ft (25.6m) and is fitted with Fowler flaps, while a distinctive feature is the tall T-tail. One consequence of pressurization is that the passenger windows are smaller. Let expects to certificate the L-610 in 1990 and to begin delivery of 600 to Aeroflot to replace the An-24 and Yak-40.

Above: CSA Czech airlines was one of numerous operators of the original L-410A, with Canadian PT6A-27 engines.

Below: The considerably larger L-610 may be built in even greater quantities than the L-410UVP. Aeroflot alone could buy 600.

LOCKHEED L-1011 TRISTAR

Above: N301EA was the second TriStar built, delivered to Eastern on 24 March 1973 (others had been delivered earlier).

Below: CS-TEE was the last of five Dash-500s for TAP, almost the last customer. It was a very different aircraft from the pioneer TriStar pictured above.

SPECIFICATION: L-1011-250 TriStar
Origin: USA.
Engines: Three 50,000lb (22,680kg) Rolls-Royce RB211-524B4 turbofans.
Dimensions: Span 155ft 4in (47.34m), (500) 164ft 4in, (50.08m); length 178ft 8in (54.45m), (500) 165ft 2in, (50.24m); wing area 3,456sq ft (321m²).
Weights: Empty, operating 249,755lb (113,289kg); max takeoff 510,000lb (231,330kg).
Performance: Cruising speed 544-575mph (875-925km/h); range (maximum payload) 5,850 miles (9,415km).
Accommodation: Typically 24+232, max 400.
History: First flight 17 November 1970, (500) 16 October 1978.

Lockheed began to study the short/medium-range trunk-route airline market in 1966, basing its work on the Chicago to Los Angeles route, with a need for the ability to use quite short runways. The design finally adopted had an engine under each wing and a third inside the end of the fuselage fed by a curved duct from above. The fuselage diameter was set at 19ft 7in (5.97m), giving an internal cabin width of 18ft 11in (5.77m), suitable for first-class seating 2+2+2 and economy seating 3+3+3. Other features included double-slotted flaps, inboard and outboard ailerons, full-span leading-edge slats, fully powered flight controls and four-wheel bogie main landing gears retracting inwards.

Lockheed picked the Rolls-Royce RB211 engine, which was giving about 38,500lb (17,464kg) thrust, and got the first L-1011 into the air in late 1970. Deliveries began, to Eastern, on 5 April 1972, but by this time there were severe problems centred on the British engine. Rolls-Royce had gone bankrupt and the RB211 was full of difficulties and severely down on power. Gradually the engine was cured, and the L-1011 saved, but lack of a high-power version of the engine enabled the rival DC-10 to dominate the market.

Lockheed was eventually able to follow the original L-1011-1 with the L-1011-100 with extra fuel, the -200 with more fuel and the RB211-524 engine rated at 48,000lb (21,773kg), and the -500 extended-range version with 50,000lb (22,680kg) engines and a further big increase in fuel capacity. The -500 also introduced a shorter fuselage and typically carries 246 passengers, the maximum being 330. The range with 246 passengers is 5,998 miles (9,653km).

Altogether Lockheed built 250 TriStars, ending in 1984. Since then the company has offered various update programmes and freighter conversions. The most complete transformation has been from early versions to the L-1011-250. Structure is strengthened and -524B4 engines fitted to enable the range to be increased by no less than 2,300 miles (3,700km).

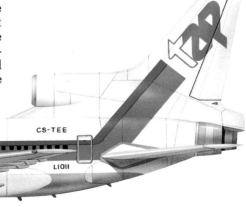

AIR PORTUGAL CS-TEE L1011

McDONNELL DOUGLAS DC-8

When Boeing launched the 707, Douglas was forced to respond even though, unlike its rival, it had no huge USAF orders to use as a launch pad for the programme. Thus the DC-8 represented a colossal financial gamble, but the aircraft was technically excellent and sold well from the very first order by PanAm on 13 October 1955.

Unlike the 707/720, every DC-8 was initially the same size, though differing in fuel capacity, weight and engine thrust. Wing sweep was 30°, compared with the 707's 35°, and Douglas claimed superior handling, especially at low speeds. The cabin environmental system had ram inlets under the nose instead of above the engines, and the passenger windows were larger.

Flight controls were powered, and an odd detail was that a portion of each inboard flap was hinged up as the flap was lowered to avoid the inboard jet.

At first Douglas offered a Domestic DC-8 weighing 211,000lb (95,710kg) and an Overwater model at 257,000lb (116,575kg), both powered by the Pratt & Whitney JT3C engine of 13,000lb (5,897kg). A few DC-8-40s were sold with the RR Conway engine which was lighter, more powerful and burned less fuel. By far the most important of the early models was the Series 50 and the Jet Trader cargo version, weighing up to 325,000lb (147,420kg) and powered by 18,000lb (8,165kg) Pratt & Whitney JT3D turbofans. Total production of the DC-8 from the Dash-10 to the Dash-55 Jet Trader amounted to 293. But Boeing had sold twice as many 707s, and Douglas inevitably found new orders hard to come by.

In April 1965 it was decided to launch the Super Sixty series, the DC-8-61 with a fuselage stretched by no less than 36ft 8in (11.18m) to increase capacity from 189 to 269, the -62 with a smaller stretch but improved low-drag wings and engine nacelles, and the -63 combining the long body with the new wings and engine pods. These transformed the programme and took sales to 556, completed in May 1972.

Everyone liked the DC-8 but it needed a long runway and was very noisy. Salvation lay in the CFM56, one of the new species of high bypass ratio fan engines. A total of 110 aircraft was re-engined as -71s or -73s.

Below: Swissair was one of the operators of the very long range DC-8-62. They were sold as the airline's A310s were delivered.

SPECIFICATION: DC-8 Super 73
Origin: USA.
Engines: Four 22,000lb (9,979kg) CFM56-2-C turbofans.
Dimensions: Span 148ft 5in (45.23m); length 187ft 4in (57.12m); wing area 2,927sq ft (271.9m²).
Weights: Empty, operating 166,500lb, (75,525kg); max takeoff 355,000lb (161,025kg).
Performance: Cruising speed 531mph (854km/h); range with max passenger payload 5,560 miles (8,950km).
Accommodation: All-tourist, up to 269 passengers.
History: First flight 30 May 1958, (Super 63) 10 April 1967, (Super 71) 15 August 1981.

Below: Air Jamaica is another airline which operated the DC-8. This Dash-62H was bought from United in 1973 and was used for several years.

Left: 9G-ACM, a DC-9-51, was one of the last Dash-51s built. Bought new in 1978, it is Ghana Airways only DC-9.

SPECIFICATION: DC-9
Origin: USA.
Engines: Two Pratt & Whitney JT8D turbofans, with ratings from 14,000 to 16,000lb (6,350 to 7,258kg).
Dimensions: Span 93ft 5in (28.47m), (except -10), 89ft 5in (27.25m); length (10, 20) 104ft 4.8in (31.82m), (30) 119ft 3.5in (36.37m), (40) 125ft 7.3in (38.28m), (50) 132ft 0in (40.3m); wing area (10) 934.3sq ft (86.77m²), (rest) 1,000.7sq ft (92.97m²).
Weights: Empty, operating (10) 45,300lb, (20,550kg), (20) 49,900lb (22,620kg), (30) 58,500lb (26,535kg), (40) 60,300lb (27,352kg), (50) 65,000lb (29,500kg); max takeoff (10) 77,700lb (35,245kg), (20) 98,000lb (44,450kg), (30) 108,000lb (48,989kg), (40) 114,000lb (51,710kg), (50) 120,000lb (54,432kg).
Performance: Cruising speed 509-561mph (819-903km/h); range (econ cruise) (10 with 50 passengers) 1,311 miles (2,110km), (20, 50 passengers) 1,843 miles (2,970km), (30, 80 passengers) 1,923 miles (3,095km), (40, 87 passengers) 1,790 miles (2,880km), (50, 97 passengers) 2,067 miles (3,326km).
Accommodation: Max passengers (10, 20) 56-90, (30) 119, (40) 132, (50) 139.
History: First flight 25 February 1965, (50) 5 July 1973.

The first DC-9 design, in 1958, looked just like a small version of the DC-8. Although it was not built, Douglas never lost sight of its wish to build a short-haul partner to the DC-8, and at last it went ahead in April 1963. The final configuration was similar to the rival One-Eleven, with a T-tail and rear-mounted engines, a low wing and very short twin-wheel landing gear.

Douglas had learned with the DC-8 that it is a bad policy to offer customers only one size of aircraft, and with the DC-9 and its successors, the MD-80/90, airlines were to be offered a greater range of cabin sizes than in any other aircraft in history. This gave the DC-9 a big advantage over the One-Eleven. Another advantage was that the JT8D engine is basically bigger than the Spey, enabling weights to be increased. Thus, Douglas has sustained a production run at Long Beach that will certainly endure for 40 years.

Below: Hawaiian uses a fleet of leased DC-9s, including this Dash-51 as well as short-bodied Dash-15 versions.

To show how fast a jetliner can be certificated, Douglas flew the first DC-9 at the end of February 1965 and obtained FAA certification less than nine months later. The first operator was Delta, but it was Eastern who – to the chagrin of Boeing who were trying to launch the 737 – first bought a stretched version.

A few DC-9s have been given the suffix C, F or RC for Convertible, Freight or Rapid Change. Three military versions of the DC-9 were also built, all based on the Dash-30. These are the USAF's C-9A Nightingale aeromedical transport, the C-9B Skytrain II of the Navy/Marines and the VC-9C VIP transport. The C-9B is the longest-ranged of all DC-9 versions and has a large side door for loading pallets of cargo. Two copies of this version were supplied to Kuwait, and another military user is the Italian Air Force.

From 1975 Douglas studied ways of making the DC-9 more fuel-efficient and less noisy, and the answer was at first called the DC-9 Super 80. Later it was restyled as the MD-80, as described opposite. Thus, production of the DC-9 came to an end with the 976th aircraft in September 1982. It is probable that many will be re-engined with the Rolls-Royce Tay.

McDONNELL DOUGLAS MD-80 & MD-90

SPECIFICATION: MD-80
Origin: USA.
Engines: Two Pratt & Whitney JT8D-209, 217 or 219 turbofans, rated at 18,500lb(8,392kg), 20,000lb (9,072kg) or 21,000lb (9,526kg) respectively.
Dimensions: Span 107ft 10in (32.87m); length 147ft 10in (45.06m), except MD-87 130ft 5in (39.75m); wing area 1,270sq ft (118m^2).
Weights: Empty, operating (81) 78,421lb, (35,571kg), (82) 78,549lb (35,629kg), (83) 80,563lb (36,543kg), (87 std fuel) 73,157lb (33,183kg); max takeoff (81, 87) 140,000lb (63,503kg), (82, 88) 149,500lb (67,812kg), (83, 88 option) 160,000lb (72,575kg).
Performance: Cruising speed (all) 500-528mph (805-850km/h); range (155 passengers) (81) 1,800 miles (2,896km), (82) 2,360 miles (3,798km), (83) 2,880 miles (4,635km), (87 with 130 passengers) 2,731 or 3,260 miles (4,395 or 5,243km).
Accommodation: Up to 172 passengers (87, up to 139).
History: First flight (Super 80) 18 October 1979, (83) 17 December 1984, (88) 15 August 1987.

In 1975 Douglas Aircraft was immersed in studies of how best to update the DC-9 to keep it in production. Almost all ideas involved a switch to the JT8D-200 series engine which is basically the original JT8D fitted with a larger fan to give more thrust with less noise and better fuel economy. The imponderables included how much (if at all) to stretch the already thrice-lengthened fuselage and whether to redesign the wing structure.

In October 1977 the decision was taken to go ahead with what was at first called the DC-9 Super 80, but was later restyled the McDonnell Douglas MD-80 as the first of the new 'MD' designations (MD-9-80 would have been more logical). This has the Dash-209 engine, a fuselage stretched (over the DC-9-50) by 14ft 3in (4.34m), almost entirely ahead of the wing, a wing extended at both the root and the tip to increase the area by 28%, a larger horizontal tail and improved furnishing in the passenger cabin.

Quite soon, different versions were offered. The original model became the MD-81, the first service being operated by Swissair on 5 October 1980. Like other versions this was later offered with engines having an emergency thrust reserve (of 750 or 850lb [340 or 386kg], depending on sub-type) which becomes available automatically in the event of engine failure. As in the DC-9, clamshell reversers are fitted, as are full-span leading-edge slats on the wings, and an electrically operated airstairs door at the front.

In 1979 Douglas announced the MD-82, unchanged in size but cleared to higher weights and fitted with the more powerful -217 engine. In 1985 this version was adopted by CAAC of China, the aircraft being assembled at Shanghai.

In 1983 Douglas offered the MD-83 with Dash-219 engines giving a slight reduction in fuel consumption, and extra tanks in the cargo compartment. Next, in 1985, came the MD-87, the only version to have a shorter fuselage. A year later Douglas followed with the MD-88, a standard-length aircraft with all the MD-87 upgrades plus a flight-management system. In 1989 the MD-90 was announced with the quieter, more efficient V2500 engine. MD-80/90 orders and options exceed 1,900.

Above: An artist's impression of the latest member of the family, the MD-90-30.

Below: HB-INE was the fifth MD-80 built, delivered to Swissair in November 1980. An MD-81, it is one of 22 signed for by the Swiss airline.

McDONNELL DOUGLAS DC-10

Like the L-1011, the DC-10 stemmed from the American Airlines specification of 1966 for a twin-engined wide-body. Again like its rival, it emerged with a third engine at the tail, though unlike the Lockheed design this was installed not in the tailcone but in a straight-through nacelle between the fuselage and fin.

Following 1960s practice, the wing was given a modest aspect ratio (7.5) and 35° sweep, an unusual feature being to pivot the double-slotted flaps on large external hinges despite the extra drag thereby caused. The fuselage width was set at 19ft 9in (6.02m), sufficient for economy seating to be arranged 3+4+3. The initial Dash-10 version made its first flight with American on 5 August 1971.

Development by General Electric of more powerful CF6 engines enabled Douglas to beat Lockheed in offering heavier long-range versions. The -15 merely had more power, for hot/high airports. The -30 introduced a longer-span wing, centreline landing gear and more fuel. The -30ER has auxiliary tanks in the aft cargo compartment and the -40 has Pratt & Whitney engines.

In its early years the DC-10 suffered a spate of accidents, attracting the attention of the media and even giving rise to passenger concern. This situation passed into history and the "Ten" took its place as a worthy member of the famed DC family.

In 1973 Douglas flew the first -30CF convertible freighter, with a large side door and provisions for various mixes of passengers and cargo. Federal Express was a customer for the DC-10-30F all-cargo version. The -30CF was the basis for the KC-10A Extender tanker/cargo aircraft, 60 of which were supplied to the USAF. Not including these, Douglas built 386 DC-10s, finishing in 1989.

SPECIFICATION: DC-10
Origin: USA.
Engines: Three turbofans, (10) 40,000lb (18,144kg) GE CF6-6D, (30) CF6-50 rated at 49,000lb (22,226kg) to 54,000lb (24,494kg), (40) P&W JT9D-20 (49,000lb (22,226kg)) or JT9D-59A (53,000lb (24,041kg)).
Dimensions: Span (10, 15) 155ft 4in (47.35m), (30, 40) 165ft 4.5in (50.4m); length (10) 181ft 5in (55.3m), (15, 30, 40) 182ft 1in (55.5m); wing area (10, 15) 3,861sq ft (358.7m²), (30, 40) 3,958sq ft (367.7m²).
Weights: Empty, basic (10) 244,903lb (111,086kg), (15) 246,547lb (111,832kg), (30) 267,197lb (121,198kg), (40) 271,062lb (122,951kg); max takeoff (10, 15) 455,000lb (206,385kg), (30) 580,000lb (263,085kg), (40) 555,000-572,000lb (251,745-259,450kg).
Performance: Cruising speed 541mph (871km/h); range (max payload) (10) 2,706 miles (4,355km), (30) 4,606 miles (7,413km), (40, -59A) 4,663 miles (7,505km).
Accommodation: Normal mixed-class 255 or 270; max (all) 380.
History: First flight 29 August 1970, (30) 21 June 1972.

Left: Takeoff by D-ADKO, one of 11 DC-10-30s of the Federal German flag carrier, Deutsche Lufthansa. They will be replaced by A340s.

Below: Air Afrique is an international carrier owned by 11 African states. It has two DC-10-30s, as well as Airbuses, 727s and DC-8s.

McDONNELL DOUGLAS MD-11

SPECIFICATION: MD-11
Origin: USA.
Engines: Three turbofans, 60,000lb (27,216kg) P&W PW4460, or 61,500lb (27,896kg) GE CF6-80C2D1F or 67,500lb (30,618kg) RR Trent 710.
Dimensions: Span 169ft 6in (51.66m); length 200ft 10in (61.21m); wing area 3,648sq ft (338.9m^2).
Weights: Empty, operating 277,500lb (125,874kg); max takeoff 602,500lb (273,289kg).
Performance: Cruising speed 544-578mph (876-930km/h); range (max payload) 5,760 miles (9,270km), ER version, 6,564 miles (10,563km).
Accommodation: Standard mixed-class seating for 323 (ER version, 277). Proposed stretched versions, up to 520.
History: First flight, 10 January 1990.

Douglas studied every possible way to improve or update the DC-10 and, in 1980-83, almost launched the MD-100 with a shorter fuselage and engines in the 35,000lb (15,876kg) class. Suddenly, in 1986, the company went ahead with high priority on the opposite tack when it conceived a stretched DC-10 with engines in the 60,000lb (27,200kg) class!

The MD-11 is basically a DC-10-30 with newer engines, a stretched fuselage, a slightly extended wing with tip winglets, a smaller tailplane with less sweep forming a trimming fuel tank, a low-drag (MD-87 type) tailcone and a modern electronic-display cockpit. Though similar in shape, many parts of the airframe have been redesigned in new alloys or composite materials. Douglas claim a 27% improvement in

Above: The second MD-11 pictured on test above the Sierra Nevada mountains. By April 1990 a total of 31 customers had signed for 344 of the initial version.

range over the DC-10-30, combined with a cut in seat/mile costs of 31%.

Despite the fact that it is not a new but a derivative aircraft, the MD-11 has proved a tremendous sales success. By mid-1990 Douglas had taken more than 340 commitments from 31 customers. Meanwhile, Douglas continues to study variants, beginning with the -11ER with extra fuel and the DC-10 length of fuselage. There are Combi and all-freight versions, as well as the MD-12 with 35ft (10.67m) of additional fuselage length, seating 90 extra passengers. With a ''Panorama Deck'' under the main floor (instead of cargo

and baggage), a maximum of 520 passengers could be carried.

Five aircraft were used in the certification programme, four having GE engines and No 3 having the PW4460. It was planned that airline service should start in 1991 (these dates being a year behind the original schedule). Launch customer for the Trent-engined version is Air Europe and this is due for certification in 1993.

Below: Air Europe, a British operator, has bought MD-11s to add to its fleets of Boeings and Fokker 100s. They will have Trent engines.

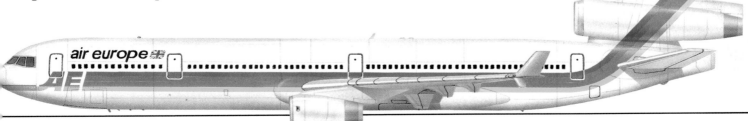

SAAB 340

SPECIFICATION: Saab 340
Origin: Sweden.
Engines: Two 1,735shp (1,293kW) GE CT7-5A2 turboprops (340B, 1,870shp (1,393kW) CT7-9B).
Dimensions: Span 70ft 4in (21.44m); length 64ft 8.5in (19.72m); wing area 450sq ft (41.81m^2).
Weights: Empty, operating 17,415lb (7,899kg); max takeoff (340) 28,000lb (12,700kg), (340B) 28,500lb (12,927kg).
Performance: Cruising speed (340) 288-313mph (463-504km/h), (340B) 325mph (522 km/h); range max payload (340) 725 miles (1,167km), (340B) 1,123 miles, (1,807km).
Accommodation: Up to 35 passengers.
History: First flight 25 January 1983.

Above: Norwegian airline A/S Norving has 340s as well as five other kinds of small twin-turboprop.

This attractive twin-turboprop was originally the Saab-Fairchild SF-340 but in 1985 the US partner passed control to the Swedish company. Fairchild remained responsible for the wings, tail and engine nacelles but, in 1987, pulled out entirely, leaving the aircraft all-Swedish.

Foreign contributors include General Electric of the USA for the engines, Dowty Rotol of Britain for the advanced slow-turning propellers with four composite blades, AP Precision of Britain for the twin-wheel landing gears, HamStan of the USA for the pressurization/environmental system, Collins for the digital avionics and flight-guidance system and Lucas for the electroluminescent instruments. All leading edges have pneumatic inflatable boot deicers. Saab

assemble and test 340s but Metair of England handles the furnishing and customer completion.

Standard seating is 2+1 for 34 or 35 passengers. Scheduled service began with Crossair on 14 June 1984. In 1985 slightly more powerful engines were fitted, driving propellers enlarged from 10ft 6in to 11ft (3.2-3.35m).

In late 1987 Saab announced the go-ahead on the 340B. This has more powerful engines, a larger tailplane and increased weights. The B version has better hot/high altitude perform-

ance and longer range. Both versions have sold well to airlines and corporate customers, the total of firm orders by May 1990 exceeding 300.

In 1988 Saab announced the larger, 50-seat Saab 2000. This will have 3,650shp (2,720kW) Allison GMA 2100 engines driving six-blade propellers, and will cruise at 414mph (667km/h).

Below: The first 340 prototype was painted in the markings of Crossair of Switzerland, the first customer.

SHORTS 330 & 360

Having established production of the rough and simple Skyvan utility aircraft, Shorts of Belfast reasoned that its cabin – 6ft 4in (1.93m) wide and high – ought to be suitable for an attractive, simple airliner. The result was the Shorts 330 which entered service in 1976. Powered by more powerful versions of the same turboprop as used in the Let L-410 and Bandeirante, the 330 cost little more per mile than those smaller aircraft but carried 30 passengers instead of about 18!

Lack of pressurization proved no problem at all (a passenger survey showed that most passengers thought it was pressurized). The simplicity reduced costs while the square-section cabin enabled passengers to sit 2+2 with ample headroom. The latter also

Below: SX-BGA to BGF are the six Shorts 330s of Olympic Airways of Greece. They are shorter than the 360 and have a twin-finned tail.

made possible stewardess service which is impossible in such cramped aircraft as the two previously mentioned, or others like them. Sales are now slow, having been overtaken by the 360, but in 1990 they exceeded the 180 mark. This total includes the Sherpa freighter version.

Shorts then took the obvious next step in picking a new version of the PT6A engine, uprated from 1,198 to 1,424shp (893 to 1,060kW), enabling the fuselage to be stretched to seat 36. The stretch improves the appearance of the new aircraft, the 360, and this was further enhanced by fitting a new tail with a swept single fin. Wing span is very slightly increased, but the wings and bracing struts are strengthened to enable weight to increase by nearly 7,000lb (3,175kg).

Shorts built the first 360 amazingly quickly. Certification was obtained in 1982 and acceptance by customers was immediate – Suburban Airlines of the

SPECIFICATION: Shorts 360
Origin: UK.
Engines: Two 1,424shp (1,061kW) P&W Canada PT6A-65AR or -67R turboprops.
Dimensions: Span 74ft 9.5in (22.8m); length 70ft 9.6in (21.58m); wing area 454sq ft (42.18m²).
Weights: Empty, operating 17,350lb (7,870kg); max takeoff 27,100lb (12,292kg).
Performance: Cruising speed 249mph (400km/h); range with 31 passengers and reserves 732 miles (1,178km).
Accommodation: 36 (optionally 39) passengers.
History: First flight 1 June 1981.

USA flew the first service in December 1982. Initial deliveries had the -65R engine of 1,294shp (964kW), driving the same five-blade Hartzell propeller as fitted to the 330. In 1985 the engine was switched to the more powerful PT6A-65AR derivative, and today the Shorts 360-300 is fitted with quieter six-blade propellers plus a number of other updates.

Below: British Midland called the Shorts 360 "The equipment that turned losses into profits". The British Midland Group has 11, some operated by associate companies Manx and Loganair.

TUPOLEV Tu-134

SPECIFICATION: Tu-134A
Origin: Soviet Union.
Engines: Two 14,990lb (6,800kg) Soloviev D-30-II turbofans.
Dimensions: Span 95ft 1.7in (29.0m); length 121ft 6.5in (37.05m); wing area 1,370.3sq ft (127.3m^2).
Weights: Empty, operating 64,045lb (29,050kg); max takeoff 103,615lb (47,000kg).
Performance: Cruising speed 466-550mph (750-885km/h); range at 750km/h with max payload 1,174 miles (1,890km).
Accommodation: Normally 12+56, but up to 96 high-density.
History: First flight believed 1963,(134A) believed 1969.

Thanks to the ease with which the Tu-16 twin-jet bomber could be adapted with a passenger fuselage, the Soviet Union was the second country to put a jet airliner into service. This was the Tu-104 in 1956. Large numbers were built, followed by a smaller version, the Tu-124, but after 1960 these were becoming obsolescent. The Tu-134 was their replacement.

The Tupolev design bureau improved the circular-section fuselage, putting the sharply swept wing completely under the floor so that the cabin could be all at one level. A glazed 'bomber' nose was retained for the navigator, the weather/navigation radar being underneath. New turbofan engines were designed and these were mounted at the rear, driving constant-speed AC generators. This in turn called for a T-type tail.

In keeping with Aeroflot requirements the landing gear was given four-wheel bogies matched to rough airstrips, and the Tupolev practice was continued of retracting these bogies aft into large fairings. Hydraulic spoilers were fitted, but the leading edge was fixed. Hot-air deicing was provided for the wing and fin, the tailplane being heated electrically.

Production at Kharkov switched in late 1970 to the Tu-134A, with a 6ft 11in (2.1m) fuselage stretch to add two rows of seats, increasing maximum capacity from 72 to 80. D-30 Series II engines were fitted, with reversers.

Other new features in the 134A included stronger landing gear, improved brakes and new avionics to meet international radio and navigation standards. The third of a batch of six 134As for Aviogenex of Yugoslavia

Above: CSA (Czech airlines) still operates 13 Tu-134As but will very soon replace them by quieter and more efficient aircraft.

was completed with a conventional airline nose, with the radar replacing the glazed navigator station. This became the preferred nose on subsequent production and was fitted to a few Tu-134s previously in service.

Later, the Tu-134B was introduced with a forward-facing cockpit (the navigator or engineer occupying a jump seat between the pilots). In the 134B-3 new lightweight seats allowed maximum passenger capacity to be increased to 96. Total production of 134s exceeded 700, many being exported.

Below: The Polish state airline LOT is about to retire its seven-strong fleet of Tupolev Tu-134As after many years of service.

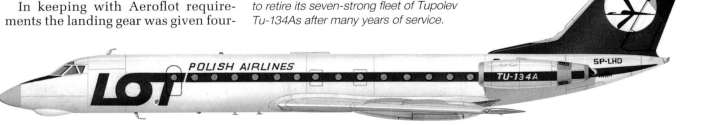

TUPOLEV Tu-154

SPECIFICATION: Tu-154M
Origin: Soviet Union.
Engines: Three 23,380lb (10,605kg) Soloviev D-30KU-154-II turbofans.
Dimensions: Span 123ft 2.5in (37.55m); length 157ft 1.8in (47.9m); wing area 2,169sq ft (201.45m²).
Weights: Empty, operating 121,915lb (55,300kg); max takeoff 220,460lb (100,000kg).
Performance: Cruising speed up to 590mph (950km/h); range (at 497mph, (800km/h), max payload) 2,425 miles (3,900km).
Accommodation: Various configurations up to max 180 passengers.
History: First flight 4 October 1968, (154M) 1982.

Announced in 1966, the Tu-154 is a fairly close equivalent to the Boeing 727-200. It is bigger and more powerful, but was originally lighter, entering service with a takeoff run of 3,740ft (1,140m), compared with about 8,000ft (2,440m) for the 727.

It was particularly designed to operate from rough airports and to replace the Tu-104 jet and the An-10 and Il-18 turboprops. In many ways it resembles an enlarged version of the Tu-134, though with a third engine in the rear fuselage, fed via an S-duct from an inlet ahead of the fin. Wing sweep is 35° and the wing has hot-air deicing of the leading edge, in front of which are electrically heated slats. As in the 727, the flaps are triple-slotted. Hot air is again used to de-ice the tail and engine inlets. All flight controls are fully powered; and the wings are fitted with spoilers for roll control and for use as airbrake/dumpers.

To spread the load on poor surfaces each main landing gear has a six-wheel bogie. Each unit retracts hydraulically into a typical Tupolev fairing aft of the wing. The Tu-154 took a long time to develop, and regular passenger service did not begin until 1972, seating 130 mixed-class or 160 high-density. The engine was the 20,950lb (9,500kg) Kuznetsov NK-8-2.

In 1975 Aeroflot began operating the Tu-154A, with 23,150lb (10,500kg) NK-8-2U engines. These allowed takeoff weight to rise from 185,188lb to 207,235lb (94,000kg), enabling more fuel to be carried with maximum pay-load. Other changes included the use of three AC electrical systems.

In 1977 production began of the Tu-154B, soon redesignated B-2 with a French automatic flight control and navigation system able to land in bad visibility. Other changes included increased fuel capacity and improved furnishings, increasing seating to 180. The Tu-154C is a cargo version with a larger forward door and special pallet handling system.

In 1984 deliveries began from Kuibyshev of the Tu-154M. This has Soloviev engines, the centre-engine inlet being enlarged. The tailplane is redesigned, the slats smaller and the spoilers enlarged. About 120 have been built, following on from over 600 of the earlier versions.

Below: MALEV, the state airline of Hungary, operates a fleet of ten Tu-154/154B aircraft. The six-wheel bogies are just visible here.

Below: The Tu-154 is similar in appearance to the Boeing 727-200, with three rear mounted engines. The airliner was designed to operate from rough airports with runways of compacted earth and gravel.

MALEV ≣ HUNGARIAN AIRLINES

HA-LCM

The Tu-204 was one of three new Soviet airliners announced in 1986 (the others being the Il-96 and Il-114). It is a very close equivalent to the Boeing 757, though the Soviet aircraft has a more efficient wing of greater span and higher aspect ratio (9.59 against 7.79), considerably lighter weights, lower fuel capacity and shorter range.

Cabin width is 11ft 8½in (3.57m) about 2in (5cm) wider than the 757, though the US aircraft can accommodate more passengers. Reflecting increased use of jetways (loading bridges) at major airports, the 204 has passenger doors high above the ground at the front and rear.

The engines are of the new and very efficient type also fitted to the Il-96. They are installed in nacelles with full-length fan ducts made of composite material, with reversers handling both hot and cold flows. The pods are toed inwards (as on the wing engines of the MD-11 but not the DC-10).

The wing has track-mounted double-slotted flaps, full-span slats, multiple-function spoilers and small conventional ailerons. Sweepback is 28°, and tip winglets are fitted. The tailplane is mounted on the fuselage, with dihedral, and forms a trimming fuel tank. A high proportion of composites is used throughout the airframe.

All flight controls are fully powered, with electrical (fly by wire) signalling. The advanced avionics include triplex circuits to allow blind automatic landings. The Tu-204 can be flown by two pilots but Aeroflot still require a flight engineer as well as a fourth seat. Each pilot has three colour electronic displays and a conventional type of control handwheel.

Tupolev have now offered two heavier 204 options. The first will weigh 219,355lb (99,500kg), and will enable a full load of 196 passengers to fly 3,293 miles (5,300km). The second, at 237,875lb (107,900kg) has more fuel for a range of 4,460 miles (7,177km).

SPECIFICATION: Tu-204
Origin: Soviet Union.
Engines: Two 35,275lb (16,000kg) Soloviev PS-90A turbofans.
Dimensions: Span 137ft 9.5in (42.0m); length 151ft 7.7in (46.22m); wing area 1,982.5sq ft (184.17m²).
Weights: Empty, operating 124,560lb (56,500kg); max takeoff 206,125lb (93,500kg).
Performance: (estimated, max wt) cruising speed 503-528mph (810-850km/h); range with maximum payload 1,553 miles (2,500km).
Accommodation: Various configurations up to max high-density of 214 passengers.
History: First flight 2 January 1989.

Above: The Tu-204 was unpainted when it made its first flight, but the same aircraft was in full Aeroflot livery by the time it appeared at the Paris air show in June 1989.

Below: The Tu-204 is a good-looking aircraft, with a specification that is not very different (apart from range) from that of the Boeing 757.

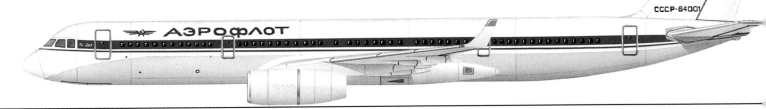

YAKOVLEV Yak-42

As has often been the case with Soviet civil transports, the Yak-42 has taken some time to perfect, ten years having elapsed between first flight and sustained service with Aeroflot. Though a jet, it was required to operate from primitive airports without paved runways or any other facilities in the world's severest climates ranging from the scorching deserts of the southern republics to the arctic conditions of northern Siberia.

The Yakovlev design bureau had already produced the Yak-40 for such work, but the Yak-42 is much bigger and heavier. The wing is swept 23° and has full-span droop flaps on the leading edge and single-slotted flaps, plus spoilers and powered ailerons. The T-type tail has powered elevators and rudder, and the tailplane can be driven through a range of 12° for trimming.

The fuselage has a circular section with a diameter of 12ft 5½in (3.66m) sufficient for 3+3 seating. The accommodation is pressurized and air-conditioning on the ground can be provided by the APU (auxiliary power unit) which also provides power for engine starting. Powered airstair doors are fitted under the tail and on the left side behind the cockpit.

The completely new three-shaft engines are grouped at the back, without reversers, the centre engine being fed by an S-duct from a sloping inlet ahead of the fin. The Yak-42 was designed to takeoff on any two engines and continue level flight on one. The

D-36 complies with international legislation on noise and smoke. Integral tanks in the wings house 5,100 Imp gal (23,175l) of fuel.

The prototypes had twin-wheel main landing gears but these were changed to four-wheel bogies in the production version to improve behaviour on soft surfaces. These retract inward, flat discs being attached to the exposed wheels because there are doors over the leg only.

As late as 1985 changes were being introduced. For example, on the Yak-42M, the wing span was increased by 19in (48cm), and maximum weight by 1,102lb (500kg). Updates were also being introduced to the avionics to improve navigation and the ability to land in bad weather.

Production and assembly is centred at a factory at Smolensk.

Below: Several recent Soviet civil transports have suffered long and difficult development, and this was certainly true of the Yak-42. Today, the problems seem to be over.

Above: Aircraft 42306 was one of the first Yak-42s to be delivered, as long ago as 1978. Since then consecutive numbers have been seen up to 42393 and Aeroflot expects to get 200 to replace Tupolev Tu-134s.

SPECIFICATION: Yak-42
Origin: Soviet Union.
Engines: Three 14,330lb (6,500kg) Lotarev D-36 turbofans, (42M, 16,535lb (7,500kg) D-436).
Dimensions: Span 114ft 5.2in (34.88m); length 119ft 4.3in (36.38m); wing area 1,615sq ft (150m²).
Weights: Empty, equipped 76,236lb (34,580kg); max takeoff (42) 124,560lb (56,500kg), (42M) 145,505lb (66,000kg).
Performance: Cruising speed 460-503mph (740-810km/h); range with 120 passengers (42) 1,180 miles (1,900km), (42M) 2,330 miles (3,750km).
Accommodation: Usually 96+8 passengers or, one-class, 120.
History: First flight 7 March 1975.

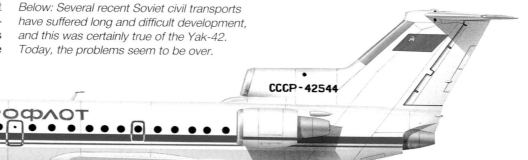

INDEX

PRINTED IN BELGIUM BY
proost
INTERNATIONAL BOOK PRODUCTION